GALATIANS

J. Vernon McGee

THOMAS NELSON PUBLISHERS

Nashville

Published in Nashville, Tennessee, by Thomas Nelson, Inc.

Scripture quotations are from the KING JAMES VERSION of the Bible.

Library of Congress Cataloging-in-Publication Data

McGee, J. Vernon (John Vernon), 1904–1988
    [Thru the Bible with J. Vernon McGee]
    Thru the Bible commentary series / J. Vernon McGee.
      p.   cm.
    Reprint. Originally published: Thru the Bible with J. Vernon McGee. 1975.
    Includes bibliographical references.
    ISBN 0-7852-1050-4 (TR)
    ISBN 0-8407-3298-8 NRM
    1. Bible—Commentaries. I. Title.
BS491.2.M37 1991
220.7'7—dc20   90–41340
                                            CIP

Printed in the United States of America
10 11 12 13 - 03 02 01 00

CONTENTS

GALATIANS

PREFACE

The radio broadcasts of the Thru the Bible Radio five-year program were transcribed, edited, and published first in single-volume paperbacks to accommodate the radio audience.

There has been a minimal amount of further editing for this publication. Therefore, these messages are not the word-for-word recording of the taped messages which went out over the air. The changes were necessary to accommodate a reading audience rather than a listening audience.

These are popular messages, prepared originally for a radio audience. They should not be considered a commentary on the entire Bible in any sense of that term. These messages are devoid of any attempt to present a theological or technical commentary on the Bible. Behind these messages is a great deal of research and study in order to interpret the Bible from a popular rather than from a scholarly (and too-often boring) viewpoint.

We have definitely and deliberately attempted "to put the cookies on the bottom shelf so that the kiddies could get them."

The fact that these messages have been translated into many languages for radio broadcasting and have been received with enthusiasm reveals the need for a simple teaching of the whole Bible for the masses of the world.

I am indebted to many people and to many sources for bringing this volume into existence. I should express my special thanks to my secretary, Gertrude Cutler, who supervised the editorial work; to Dr. Elliott R. Cole, my associate, who handled all the detailed work with the publishers; and finally, to my wife Ruth for tenaciously encouraging me from the beginning to put my notes and messages into printed form.

Solomon wrote, ". . . of making many books there is no end; and much study is a weariness of the flesh" (Eccl. 12:12). On a sea of books that flood the marketplace, we launch this series of THRU THE BIBLE with the hope that it might draw many to the one Book, *The Bible*.

J. Vernon McGee

The Epistle to the
GALATIANS

INTRODUCTION

This epistle was probably written by Paul (Gal. 1:1) about A.D. 57, on the third missionary journey from Ephesus during his two years of residence there. There is substantial basis, however, for the claim that it was written from Corinth, shortly before Paul wrote the Epistle to the Romans. Dr. Lenski advances the theory that it was written from Corinth on the second missionary journey about April, A.D. 53. After Paul visited the Galatians, he discovered that the Judaizers had followed him and the churches were listening to them. Paul wrote this letter to counteract their message and to state clearly the gospel.

Paul visited the Galatian churches on each of his three missionary journeys. There is no mention in the epistle of another visit to the churches. This epistle was evidently Paul's last word to these churches, written after he had visited them on his third missionary journey.

In the case of the Epistle to the Galatians, the *people* to whom it was sent are important, which is not always true with other epistles. Also, the destination of this book has given rise to what is known as the North Galatian and the South Galatian theories. It seems more reasonable to suppose that it was sent to the churches in the area Paul visited on his first missionary journey, but this does not preclude the possibility that it had a wider circulation, even as far north as Pessinus, Ancyra, and Tavium. I believe that Paul was writing to *all* the churches of Galatia. This area was large and prominent and many churches had been established there.

The word *Galatians* could be used either in an ethnographic sense, which would refer to the nationality of the people, or it could be used in a geographic sense, which would refer to the Roman province by that name. Regardless of the position which is taken, there was a common blood strain which identified people in that area where there was a mixture of population. The people for whom the province was named were Gauls, a Celtic tribe from the same stock which inhabited France. In the fourth century B.C. they invaded the Roman Empire and sacked Rome. Later they crossed into Greece and captured Delphi in 280 B.C. They were warlike people and on the move. At the invitation of Nikomedes I, King of Bithynia, they crossed over into Asia Minor to help him in a civil war. They soon established themselves in Asia Minor. They liked it there. The climate was delightful, and the country was beautiful. When I visited Turkey, I was pleasantly surprised to find how lovely it is along the Aegean and inland, also along the Mediterranean.

In 189 B.C. these Celtic tribes were made subjects of the Roman Empire and became a province. Their boundaries varied, and for many years they retained their customs and own language. They actually were blond Orientals. The churches Paul established on his first missionary journey were included at one time in the territory of Galatia, and this is the name which Paul would normally give to these churches.

These Gallic Celts had much of the same temperament and characteristics of the American population, that is, of those who came out of Europe or England. It is interesting to see what was said concerning my ancestors (and maybe yours). Many of these Germanic tribes were wild and fierce. Caesar said of them: "The infirmity of the Gauls is that they are fickle in their resolves, fond of change, and not to be trusted." This description fits the majority of Americans in our day. We are fickle in our resolves. We are fond of change—we want a new car every year. We like to get the magazine that is dated next week. Another described them as "frank, impetuous, impressionable, eminently intelligent, fond of show, but extremely inconstant, the fruit of excessive vanity." That is a picture of the American population today. A man runs for office and we vote for him. Then in four years we forget him. Do you remember who was president ten years ago? Or twenty years ago? We are fickle people, not very constant. I'm very happy that it was said they were eminently intelligent, because that's what we think also. And the reason for our high estimation of ourselves is the fruit of excessive vanity.

In the Book of Acts we read that the Galatians wanted to make Paul a god one day, and the next day they stoned him. What do we do? We elect a man to the presidency and then we try to kill him in office. I think it is quite interesting that our system of government has survived as long as it has.

Therefore the Epistle to the Galatians has a particular message for us because it was written to people who were like us in many ways. They had a like temper, and they were beset on every hand by cults and "isms" innumerable—which takes us, likewise, from our moorings in the gospel of grace.

1. It is a stern, severe, and solemn message (see Gal. 1:6–9; 3:1–5). It does not correct conduct as the Corinthian letters do, but it is corrective. The Galatian believers were in grave peril because the foundations of their faith were being attacked—everything was threatened.

The epistle, therefore, contains no word of commendation, praise, or thanksgiving. There is no request for prayer, and there is no mention of their standing in Christ. No one with him is mentioned by name. If you compare this epistle with the other Pauline epistles, you will see that it is different.

2. In this epistle the heart of Paul the apostle is laid bare, and there is deep emotion and strong feeling. This is his *fighting epistle*—he has on his war paint. He has no toleration for legalism. Someone has said that the Epistle to the Romans comes from the head of Paul while the Epistle to the Galatians comes from the heart of Paul. A theologian has said, "Galatians takes up controversially what Romans puts systematically."

3. This epistle is a *declaration of emancipation* from legalism of any type. It is interesting to note that legalists do not spend much time with Galatians. It is a rebuke to them. This was Martin Luther's favorite epistle. He said, "This is *my* epistle. I am wedded to it." It was on

the masthead of the Reformation. It has been called the Magna Carta of the early church. It is the manifesto of Christian liberty, the impregnable citadel, and a veritable Gibraltar against any attack on the heart of the gospel. As someone put it, "Immortal victory is set upon its brow."

This is the epistle that moved John Wesley. He came to America as a missionary to the Indians. But he made a startling discovery. He said, "I came to America to convert Indians, but who is going to convert John Wesley?" He went back to London, England, and was converted. When I was in London I had a guide take us to Aldersgate and we saw the marker that designates the place where John Wesley was converted. (His was called an "evangelical conversion," which is the only kind of conversion the Bible speaks of.) John Wesley went out to begin a revival—preaching from this Epistle to the Galatians—that saved England from revolution and brought multitudes to a saving knowledge of Christ. Wilberforce, one of his converts, had a great deal to do with the matter of child labor and the Industrial Revolution that brought about changes for the working man.

In a sense I believe this epistle has been the backbone and background for every great spiritual movement and revival that has taken place in the past nineteen hundred years. And, my friend, it will be the background for other revivals. I would like to see the Spirit of God move in our land today. I would like to hear the Epistle to the Galatians declared to America. I believe it would revolutionize lives.

4. Galatians is the strongest declaration and defense of the doctrine of *justification by faith* in or out of Scripture. It is God's polemic on behalf of the most vital truth of the Christian faith against any attack. Not only is a sinner saved by grace through faith plus nothing, but the saved sinner lives by grace. Grace is a way *to* life and a way *of* life. These two go together, by the way.

OUTLINE

I. Introduction, Chapter 1:1–10
A. Salutation—Cool Greeting, Chapter 1:1–5
B. Subject Stated—Warm Declamation, Chapter 1:6–10

II. Personal—Authority of the Apostle and Glory of the Gospel, Chapters 1:11—2:14
A. Experience of Paul in Arabia, Chapter 1:11–24
B. Experience of Paul with the Apostles in Jerusalem, Chapter 2:1–10
C. Experience of Paul in Antioch with Peter, Chapter 2:11–14

III. Doctrinal—Justification by Faith, Chapters 2:15—4:31
Faith vs. Works, Liberty vs. Bondage
A. Justification by Faith—Doctrine Stated, Chapter 2:15–21
B. Justification by Faith—Experience of Galatians, Chapter 3:1–5
C. Justification by Faith—Illustration of Abraham, Chapters 3:6—4:18
D. Justification by Faith—Allegory of Hagar and Sarai, Chapter 4:19–31

IV. Practical—Sanctification by the Spirit, Chapters 5:1—6:10
Spirit vs. Flesh, Liberty vs. Bondage
A. Saved by Faith and Living by Law Perpetrates Falling from Grace, Chapter 5:1–15
B. Saved by Faith and Walking in the Spirit Produces Fruit of the Spirit, Chapter 5:16–26
C. Saved by Faith and Fruit of the Spirit Presents Christian Character, Chapter 6:1–10

V. Autographed Conclusion, Chapter 6:11–18
A. Paul's Own Handwriting, Chapter 6:11

CHAPTER 1

*THEME: Salutation—cool greeting; subject stated—
warm declamation; Paul's experience in Arabia*

Galatians is God's polemic against legalism of every and any description. The Mosaic Law is neither discredited, despised, nor disregarded. Its majesty, perfection, demands, fullness, and purpose are maintained. Yet these very qualities make it utterly impossible for man to come this route to God. Another way is opened for man to be justified before God, a way which entirely bypasses the Mosaic Law. The new route is by faith. Justification by faith is the theme, with the emphasis upon *faith.*

Three epistles in the New Testament quote Habakkuk 2:4, "The just shall live by his faith." Romans 1:17 emphasizes *the just.* Hebrews 10:38 emphasizes *shall live.* Galatians 3:11 emphasizes *by faith.*

In Romans the emphasis is upon the fact that man apart form the Mosaic Law is justified before God by faith. In Galatians Paul is defending the gospel from those who would add law to justification by faith. Faith plus law was the thrust of Judaism. Faith plus nothing was the answer of Paul.

The Judaizers questioned Paul's authority as an apostle and his teaching that simple faith was adequate for salvation. Paul defends his apostleship and demonstrates the sufficiency of the gospel of grace to save.

SALUTATION—COOL GREETING

Paul, an apostle, (not of men, neither by man, but by Jesus Christ, and God the Father, who raised him from the dead;) [Gal. 1:1].

Actually there is no parenthesis necessary in this verse. Paul is simply stating that he is an apostle. The word *apostle* is used in a twofold sense:

1. One of the Twelve (Acts 1:21–26)
    (a) With Jesus during His three-year ministry (v. 21);
    (b) Witness of His postresurrection ministry (v. 22);
    (c) Chosen by Christ (v. 22; Acts 9:15; 26:16–17).
2. One sent forth. This is the wider sense as used in Acts 11:22.

Paul, in my judgment, took the place of Judas. After the resurrection of Jesus, Matthias was chosen by the disciples to fill the place of Judas, but no information is given about Matthias except the account given in Acts 1:15–26. Matthias is never mentioned again. If the Holy Spirit had chosen him, certainly somewhere along the way He would have set His seal upon this man. Paul, however, proved he was an apostle, and Matthias did not. The election of Matthias as an apostle was held *before* Pentecost, which was before the Holy Spirit came into the church. For that reason I do not think that the Holy Spirit had anything to do with the selection of Matthias. There are also many elections in our churches today that are obviously not ordered by the Holy Spirit. I believe that Paul is the man whom the Spirit of God chose to take Judas' place.

In this verse Paul also says that he is not "of men." The preposition *apo* conveys the meaning of "not from men," that is, it is not legalistic. He is not an apostle by appointment or commission after having attended a school or having taken a prescribed course.

Paul also declares that his apostleship is not "by man." The preposition *dia* indicates that it was not through man, that is, not ritualistic by means of laying on of hands, as by a bishop or church court. Paul did not have the other apostles lay their hands on his head and say, "Hocus pocus, you are an apostle."

Paul was an apostle. How? He was an apostle by Jesus Christ, and God the Father, who raised Him from the dead. Jesus laid His hand upon Paul, called him, and set him apart for the office (see Acts 9:15–16).

Now I am an ordained minister from men and through men. I was told that I had to finish seminary and obtain certain degrees before I could do ordained. I did that. That was from men. That was the legalistic side. Next I went before a church body that examined me. Their decision was that I should be an ordained minister. In the Second Presbyterian Church in Nashville, Tennessee, I knelt, and a group of men put their hands on me and said, "You are now an ordained minister." That is the kind of minister I am. Paul said, "I am *not* that kind of an apostle. Men had nothing to do with it. I am an apostle directly by Jesus Christ and God the Father who raised Him from the dead."

And all the brethren which are with me, unto the churches of Galatia [Gal. 1:2].

You will notice that Paul's greeting is cool, brief, formal, and terse. No one is personally mentioned. He is not writing just to one church. He is writing to several churches—"churches of Galatia."

The word *church* is used in two ways in the New Testament. One meaning of church includes the entire body of believers, of all different groups, who have trusted Christ as Savior. The other meaning of church refers to local assemblies, which is how Paul uses the word here. There were churches, or local assemblies, in many parts of Galatia. There was a church in Antioch of Pisidia, in Derbe, in Lystra, and in other places he had visited. Paul was writing to *all* the churches, to all of the local assemblies; hence the local church—not the corporate body of believers—is in view here. In the Epistle to the Ephesians we look at the church as a corporate body of believers—the invisible church. But the invisible body is to make itself visible today in a corporate body. Believers should be identified with a local body of believers.

Grace be to you and peace from God the Father, and from our Lord Jesus Christ [Gal. 1:3].

This is Paul's formal greeting that he uses in most of his epistles. The word *grace (charis)* in this verse was the gentile form of greeting in that day, while *peace (shalom)* was the religious greeting of the Jews. Now the grace of God must be experienced before the peace that is from God the Father can be experienced.

Who gave himself for our sins, that he might deliver us from this present evil world, according to the will of God and our Father [Gal. 1:4].

This is another marvelous verse—I can't rise to the level of it; I will simply say some things about it.

Jesus Christ "gave himself for our sins." There is nothing that we can add to the value of His sacrifice. Nothing! He gave Himself. What do you have to give, friend? Anything? Can you add anything to His sacrifice? He gave Himself. How wonderful and glorious that is! I am speechless when I read a verse like this. He gave Himself! When you give yourself, you have given everything—who you are, what you have, your time, your talent—everything. He gave Himself. He couldn't give any more. Paul just couldn't wait to say it. Having mentioned Him, he says, "Who gave himself for our sins." This is the germ of Paul's subject.

Paul calls Him, "*our* Lord Jesus Christ." He is *my* Savior. Can you say, "The Lord is *my* Shepherd?" It is one thing to say He is a Shepherd; it is another thing to make it possessive. The Lord is *my* Shepherd. The Lord is *my* Savior. Can you say that He is yours?

Paul goes on to say, "that he might deliver us form this present evil world." Notice that the Lord delivers us from this present evil age. There is, therefore, a present value of the gospel which proves its power and genuineness. The gospel can deliver you. I have received letters from thousands of folks who have turned to Christ and have been delivered. They have been delivered from drugs, from alcohol, and from sex sins. Christ alone can deliver in cases like that. This proves the genuineness of the gospel. Christ gave Himself for our sins. He took your place and my place on that cross. He died for us and rose from the dead "that he might deliver us from this present evil world."

All we have seen so far does not exhaust the richness of this verse.

Notice that His deliverance is "according to the will of God and our Father." He *can* deliver us—and it will not be according to law. But it must be according to the *will* of God, my friend. The will of God is that, after He has saved us, we are not to live in sin. How wonderful this is! He *can* deliver us. He *wants* to deliver us. He *will* deliver us, and He will do it according to the will of God. It is God's will that you be delivered.

This verse still is not exhausted. Christ gave Himself that He might deliver us according to the will of God. God can deliver us, but it will not be according to the Law. It must be according to the will of God, my friend. The will of God is that when He saves you, you are not to live in sin. He can deliver us and He wants to deliver us. It is His will that you be delivered. My friend, this is a verse that makes you feel like throwing your hat in the air, does it not?

To whom be glory for ever and ever. Amen [Gal. 1:5].

This is a moment wherein Paul stops to render praise to God. I am convinced that we should praise God more than we do. Let us get right down to the nitty-gritty, right down where the rubber meets the road. Did you praise the Lord's name this morning when you got up? Did you thank Him for a new day? You say, "It was raining?" But did you thank Him for it? Did you praise His name that He brought you to a new day?

I had to have a bout with cancer before I came to the place where I thank Him as I should. Now the first thing I do every morning—whether the sun is shining or it's pouring down rain—is to say, "Lord, thank you for bringing me to a new day." How wonderful He is! We need to praise Him more. I want glory to go to the name of my God and my Savior. I don't want to stand on the sidelines and compromise by endorsing these contemporary dramatic productions and songs that are belittling the Lord Jesus Christ. I am speaking out against them, because He is God manifest in the flesh. He gave Himself for me. I want to praise His name! "To whom be glory for ever and ever."

"For ever and ever" begins right now and is going on right into eternity.

This concludes Paul's salutation. Although it contains some glorious truths, I think you will have to admit that it is a cool, impersonal greeting from the apostle Paul.

SUBJECT STATED—WARM DECLAMATION

Paul now states his subject. He goes from cold to hot. In fact, he is hot under the collar. Why? Because there are those who are mutilating the gospel. Paul would give his life for the gospel.

I marvel that ye are so soon removed from him that called you into the grace of Christ unto another gospel [Gal. 1:6].

There are two aspects of the gospel, and it can be used in two senses: (1) the facts of the gospel, and (2) the interpretation of the facts. The facts of the gospel are the death, burial, and bodily resurrection of Christ. Paul said to the Corinthians, "For I delivered unto you first of all that which I also received [Paul didn't originate the gospel; he *received* it], how that Christ died for our sins according to the scriptures; And that he was buried, and that he rose again the third day according to the scriptures" (1 Cor. 15:3–4). These are the historical facts of the gospel which cannot be changed. You have never preached the gospel unless you have stated these facts. The second aspect of the gospel is the interpretation of the facts. They are to be received by faith plus nothing.

Now the subject of Paul's letter to the Galatian believers concerns the interpretation of the facts of the gospel. The Judaizers had followed Paul into the Galatian country. They did not challenge the facts of the gospel. After all, five hundred people at once saw the Lord Jesus after His resurrection. When you have that many people around as witnesses, you don't run around denying the facts of the gospel. The heresy they were promoting concerned the interpretation of those facts. They were very sly and subtle and said something like this, "Did Brother Paul come here among you?" The folk would say, "Yes, he came and preached the gospel and we accepted it. We are converted. We know Christ as our Savior, and we are in the body of believers." The Judaizers would respond, "Oh, that's wonderful. Brother Paul is accurate as far as he goes, but he doesn't go far enough. Did he tell you that you should keep the Mosaic Law? Oh, he didn't? Well, he should have told you that. Yes, you are to trust Christ, but you must also follow the Mosaic Law or you won't be saved."

This is one of the oldest heresies known, and it is still with us today. It is adding something to the gospel of grace; it is *doing* something rather than simply believing something. It is faith plus something rather than faith plus nothing. Every cult and "ism" has something for you to *do* in order to be saved.

It is interesting that Paul said to the Philippian jailer, ". . . Believe on the Lord Jesus Christ, and thou shalt be saved . . ." (Acts 16:31). Simon Peter said to the Sanhedrin, "Neither is there salvation in any other: for there is none other name under heaven given among men, whereby we must be saved" (Acts 4:12). Christ told the apostles to preach the gospel of salvation by grace. They were not to do anything to gain their salvation, but they were to trust what Christ already had done for them. The gospel shuts out all works.

Now Paul is writing to the Galatian believers and saying, "I marvel that ye are so soon removed from him that called you into the grace of Christ unto another gospel"—

> **Which is not another; but there be some that trouble you, and would pervert the gospel of Christ [Gal. 1:7].**

The word *pervert* is the Greek word *metastrephō*. It is a strong word, used by Dr. Luke in speaking of the sun *turned* to darkness (see Acts 2:20), and by James, speaking of laughter *turned* to mourning (see James 4:9). To attempt to change the gospel has the effect of making it the very opposite of what it really is. This is important to see.

> **But though we, or an angel from heaven, preach any other gospel unto you than that which we have preached unto you, let him be accursed [Gal. 1:8].**

This verse is as strong as anything could possibly be. Paul says that if an angel dared to declare any other message than the gospel, he would be dismissed with a strong invective.

If an angel should appear to me right now and say, "You are right as far as you go, but you also have to do something to be saved"; or if an angel should appear to you as you read this and say, "McGee is correct as far as he goes, but you have to do something else," both you and I should say, "Get out of here; I'm not listening to you although you are an angel from heaven."

My friend, in our day we hear many speakers who are trying to give us another "gospel." They may look like angels to you—after all, Satan himself is transformed into an angel of light, and his ministers are transformed as the ministers of righteousness (see 2 Cor. 11:14–15). Now hear Paul—

> **As we said before, so say I now again, If any man preach any other gospel unto you than that ye have received, let him be accursed [Gal. 1:9].**

In strong language Paul says, "If any man preach any other gospel unto you than that ye have received, let him be accursed," which literally means let him be damned. Friend, I cannot make that statement any stronger.

The gospel shuts out all works. Romans 4:5 says, "But to him that worketh not, but believeth on him that justifieth the ungodly, his faith is counted for righteousness." I find a great many folk who think they have to become good enough to be saved. The other day a man said to me, "McGee, I want to become a Christian. I am going to try to be a little better, and if I improve, I am going to become a Christian." I said to him, "If you improve, you will never become a Christian. The only class that God is saving is the ungodly. The Lord Jesus said He didn't come to call the righteous; He came to call sinners. The reason He said that was because there is none righteous, no, not one. Even the righteousness of man is as filthy rags in God's sight. Law condemns us, and it must make us speechless before grace can save us."

Romans 3:19 tells us that, "Now we know that what things soever the law saith, it saith to them who are under the law: that every mouth may be stopped, and all the world may become guilty before God." The real difficulty is not that people should be "good enough" to be saved, but that they are not "bad enough" to be saved. Humanity refuses to recognize its lost condition before God. This is the human predicament.

The Judaizers did not deny the facts of the gospel—that Jesus died and rose again. What they denied was that this was adequate. They insisted that you have to keep the Law plus trusting Christ. Paul is saying that whoever tries to mingle law and grace—let him be damned! Why? Because they pervert the gospel. They do not deny the fact of the gospel, but they misinterpret those facts. They pervert the gospel.

> **For do I now persuade men, or God? or do I seek to please men? for if I yet pleased men, I should not be the servant of Christ [Gal. 1:10].**

The word *persuade* means "to make a friend of." The *Scofield Reference Bible* translates it "seek the favor of." In 1 Thessalonians 2:4 and 4:1 it is "please God" in contrast to self or others. The preaching of the gospel is not pleasing to lost man. No man can please both God and man.

If you preach the gospel of grace today, you may get into trouble because it is the gospel of the grace of God that the sinner hates. Many unsaved church members do not want to hear the message of grace. They want to hear a message that appeals to the flesh. The gospel of grace puts us in the dust and makes us beggars before God.

By nature man responds to legalism. He thinks he doesn't need a Savior. All he needs is a helper. Oh, my friend, we are sinking for the third time! We need somebody to *save* us. Those who preach law are popular. Not long ago I listened to a local Southern California preacher on television. From a technical and professional standpoint he has one of the finest programs. In his message he talked about Jesus coming into the world. He spoke of Christ's death and resurrection. But he failed to mention that the people to whom he was speaking were sinners and needed a Savior. He neglected to inform his audience that Jesus died for them and they needed to trust Him to be saved. Rather, he talked about commitment. He invited folk to commit their lives to Christ. Let us be honest, friend. Christ does not want your old life and He does not want mine. We have nothing to commit to Him. He wants to do something through us today. Oh, if only we could learn that!

God is not even asking you to live the Christian life. In fact, you cannot live it. God is asking that He might live the Christian life through you. The Epistle to the Galatians teaches this. But first of all we must come to Christ as sinners and be saved. Our churches are filled today with people who are not saved. Do you know why? They have never come to Christ and received Him as Savior. They feel like they have something to commit to Him. You have *nothing* to commit to Him, my friend. He wants to commit something to you. He is the One who died, and He is on the giving end. "For the wages of sin is death; but the gift of God is eternal life through Jesus Christ our Lord" (Rom. 6:23). It is just as simple as that. Have you accepted Jesus Christ as your Savior? This is the important thing.

Man's conscience witnesses to the law, and legal conviction will lead to works. Man tries to compensate for the fact that he is not doing enough. He tries to balance his good works against his sins and have enough on the plus side to be saved. The apostle Paul, you recall, tried to do this. And he had a whole lot on the plus side. But one day he came to Christ. Then he said, "What was gain for me became loss, and what was loss became gain" (see Phil. 3:7–8).

The Holy Spirit witnesses to grace today. This is gospel conviction that leads to faith. Actually the law denies the fall of man—this was the position of Cain. Grace acknowledges the fall of man, as Abel did when he brought his offering to God.

We come now to a new section that deals with the apostle Paul personally—his experience in Arabia, his experience with the apostles in Jerusalem, and his experience in Antioch with Peter. This will take us through the first half of chapter 2.

PERSONAL—PAUL'S EXPERIENCE IN ARABIA

But I certify you, brethren, that the gospel which was preached of me is not after man [Gal. 1:11].

Paul is stating once again, as he did in verse 1, that he is a God-appointed apostle. When he says, "I certify you," he means, "I remind you." "After man" should be "according to man." Paul did not get the gospel he preached from man. The Judaizers not only questioned Paul's message, they also questioned his apostleship. He was not one of the original Twelve, but a Johnny-come-lately. They cast a shadow upon the validity of Paul's authority as an apostle. Paul is going to take up this matter with them and show that his apostleship rests upon the fact that he was called directly by the revelation of Jesus Christ.

> **For I neither received it of man, neither was I taught it, but by the revelation of Jesus Christ [Gal. 1:12].**

Paul did not receive his apostleship by going to school. Neither did he receive it by being ordained or by hands being laid on his head. Paul's apostleship and gospel came directly by a revelation (*apokalupsis*) of Jesus Christ. The Book of Revelation, sometimes called the Apocalypse, is from the same word. The gospel is a revelation as much as is the Book of Revelation. The gospel was unveiled to the apostle Paul. He did not become an apostle through Peter, James, or John. He was an apostle by the direct call of Jesus Christ.

> **For ye have heard of my conversation in time past in the Jews' religion, how that beyond measure I persecuted the church of God, and wasted it:**
>
> **And profited in the Jews' religion above many my equals in mine own nation, being more exceedingly zealous of the traditions of my fathers [Gal. 1:13–14].**

Paul says, "For ye have heard of my conversation," that is, you have heard of my manner of life. Paul now calls the religion in which he was brought up the "Jews' religion." Paul was saved, not in Judaism, but *from* Judaism.

Now notice this tremendous statement:

> **But when it pleased God, who separated me from my mother's womb, and called me by his grace,**
>
> **To reveal his Son in me, that I might preach him among the heathen; immediately I conferred not with flesh and blood:**
>
> **Neither went I up to Jerusalem to them which were apostles before me; but I went into Arabia, and returned again unto Damascus [Gal. 1:15–17].**

The phrase "but when it pleased God," in verse 15, means that Paul was called according to the will of God. The word *heathen* in verse 16 refers to Gentiles. Paul conferred not with flesh and blood—he didn't get it from any man. Paul received the gospel directly from Jesus Christ.

Many years ago a so-called modernist, who taught old heresy, wrote a book about Paul. He also gave lectures, which I heard. He gave the apostle Paul credit for being a great brain. (I personally believe Paul had the greatest mind of any man who has ever lived. Many scholars, who are better acquainted with Paul than I am also make this statement.) He pointed out that Paul was a brilliant student of the Mosaic system of Judaism and was a brilliant student of Greek philosophy, and then declared that Paul combined the two and came up with Christianity. Now Paul says here in Galatians that he didn't get the gospel that way. He received the gospel by direct revelation from Jesus Christ.

> **Then after three years I went up to Jerusalem to see Peter, and abode with him fifteen days [Gal. 1:18].**

I suppose that this verse is the same record that is given in Acts 9:26–29 which says, "And when Saul was come to Jerusalem, he assayed to join himself to the disciples: but they were all afraid of him, and believed not that he was a disciple. But Barnabas took him, and brought him to the apostles, and declared unto them how he had seen the Lord in the way, and that he had spoken to him, and how he had preached boldly at Damascus in the name of Jesus. And he was with them coming in and going out at Jerusalem. And he spake boldly in the name of the Lord Jesus, and disputed against the Grecians: but they went about to slay him."

When all of this is added up, it means that Paul spent less than three years in the desert. It is interesting how God has trained His men. He trained Moses in the desert. He put Abraham in a rather unique place to train him, and Elijah had that same type of experience. It has been God's method to put His man out on the desert to train him. David was trained outdoors in the caves of the earth while he was running away from King Saul. Remember that he cried out to God that he was hunted like a partridge—it was open season on him all the time. The Lord used the same method with Paul. God sent him into the desert for less than three years. Then he went to Jerusalem, saw Peter, and stayed with him for fifteen days.

But other of the apostles saw I none, save James the Lord's brother [Gal. 1:19].

Paul had no contact with the apostles except Peter and James, the Lord's brother. That is all the contact he had with them, and he received nothing from them, as we shall see.

Now the things which I write unto you, behold, before God, I lie not [Gal. 1:20].

The modernist or liberal to whom I referred said that Paul got his gospel by making an homogenized stew out of Greek philosophy and the Mosaic system. Paul says here that he didn't get the gospel from anyone else. Paul also says he does not lie. Someone is lying. I am too polite to call that modernist a liar, but in effect Paul does.

Afterwards I came into the regions of Syria and Cilicia;

And was unknown by face unto the churches of Judaea which were in Christ:

But they had heard only, That he which persecuted us in times past now preacheth the faith which once he destroyed.

And they glorified God in me [Gal. 1:21–24].

The believers in Jerusalem were rather reluctant to accept the apostle Paul. Without the help of Barnabas, Paul would probably have waited a long time before the church in Jerusalem would have received him. These men were hesitant to receive Paul because he had persecuted the church, but they knew what it was to be converted. They knew what it was to have an absolutely earth-shaking experience that would transform a man. Yet they could not believe that Saul of Tarsus could be converted. It seemed not only improbable but impossible.

In verses 21–24 Paul outlines his first years after his conversion. I don't think, friend, that they were the happiest years of his life. Apparently he tells us something about the failure in his own personal life in the seventh chapter of Romans. There were three periods in the life of the apostle Paul. Notice briefly the first two periods.

1. Paul was a proud Pharisee. He had a marvelous mind and was an expert in the Mosaic Law. As many of his biographers have said, the world would have heard of Paul even if he had not been an apostle and even if he had not been converted. I don't think there is any question about that. He was an outstanding man. But he was a proud young Pharisee who thought he knew it all. He hated Christ. He hated the church and attempted to eliminate it. He was ruthless in his persecution of the church.

2. The second period began on the Damascus road when he was knocked down into the dust. This brilliant Pharisee found out that he did not know Jesus Christ, whom to know is life. He had thought Jesus was dead. And he asked, "Who art thou, Lord?" Jesus replied, "I am Jesus whom you persecute. When you persecute My church, you persecute Me" (see Acts 9:5). When Paul became acquainted with his Lord, he immediately asked, "Lord, what wilt thou have me to do?" After Paul met Christ, he spent some time in Arabia. During those first years he attempted to minister and found that what he wanted to do he

could not do. Finally he cried out, "O wretched man that I am! who shall deliver me from the body of this death?" (Rom. 7:24). It was not an unsaved man who said that; it was Paul the apostle in the first stages of his conversion.

3. Then came that glorious period when he walked in the Spirit. That was the time he could live for God. That is the place where many of us need to be today. There are so many unhappy Christians. They are saved, I think, but as Dwight L. Moody put it in his quaint way, "Some people have just enough religion to make them miserable."

I wish we had more information on Paul's experience with the apostles in Jerusalem. I am sure a question has already come to your mind. If Paul received the gospel apart from the other apostles—who were with the Lord for three years and saw the resurrected Christ—is Paul preaching the same gospel? This is an important matter at this point because if Paul is not preaching the same gospel, something is radically wrong. In the next chapter we shall see that the apostles in Jerusalem approved Paul's gospel and that it was the same Good News.

CHAPTER 2

THEME: Experience of Paul with the apostles in Jerusalem; experience of Paul in Antioch with Peter; justification by faith stated

Now we come to the second division of this personal section in Galatians. We have seen that the Lord Jesus Christ communicated the gospel directly to Paul. Was it the same gospel that the other apostles had received from the lips of the Lord? We will see the oneness of the gospel and Paul's experience with the apostles in Jerusalem. We will see the communication of the gospel and see that the church in Jerusalem approved Paul's gospel.

EXPERIENCE OF PAUL WITH THE APOSTLES IN JERUSALEM

Then fourteen years after I went up again to Jerusalem with Barnabas, and took Titus with me also [Gal. 2:1].

It was a master stroke of Paul to take Titus with him. Titus was a young preacher and a Gentile. This, I believe, was the first great council in Jerusalem as recorded in Acts 15. The question to be settled was whether men are saved by the grace of God, or whether they should come in under the Mosaic Law. Paul had Titus there as exhibit number one. Titus had not been circumcised. Will he be forced to become circumcised? This was to become a very important matter.

You see, the Judaizers were going about saying that the church in Jerusalem held that all believers in Christ should be under the Mosaic Law. All of the men there at the Jerusalem church, which was an all-Jewish church, had certainly been under it. Many of them still went to the temple to worship. In fact, that must have been the Christian's meeting place. Paul and Barnabas came there to get the official word regarding law and grace.

> And I went up by revelation, and communicated unto
> them that gospel which I preach among the Gentiles,
> but privately to them which were of reputation, lest by
> any means I should run, or had run, in vain [Gal. 2:2].

Paul recognized that if he were preaching a different gospel from what
the other apostles were preaching, there was something radically
wrong. Paul was willing to admit, "If I were preaching a different gospel, I would be wrong. I have run in vain. I have certainly been disillu-
sioned and misinformed." So he goes to Jerusalem and communicates
that gospel to the apostles there.

> But neither Titus, who was with me, being a Greek, was
> compelled to be circumcised:

> And that because of false brethren unawares brought in,
> who came in privily to spy out our liberty which we
> have in Christ Jesus, that they might bring us into bond-
> age [Gal. 2:3–4].

Out where Paul was preaching some folk had come into the church
under false colors. Apparently they were not believers. They just came
in to spy out the liberty which believers had in Christ. They found out
that this young preacher, Titus, was a Greek and Paul had not com-
pelled him to be circumcised. So what will the church at Jerusalem
decide about him? Paul says, "Well, they didn't compel him to be
circumcised. They didn't listen to the false brethren. If they had, we
would be put right back under the bondage of the Mosaic Law rather
than enjoying the freedom by the Spirit of God and the freedom of
Christ."

> To whom we gave place by subjection, no, not for an
> hour; that the truth of the gospel might continue with
> you [Gal. 2:5].

Paul stood by his guns. These false brethren said, "This man Titus
who is here meeting with the church (and it was practically all Jewish

then) has not even been circumcised!" Paul says, "No, and he's not going to be circumcised. He is as much a believer as any of you. He has been saved by faith apart from the Law. He is not about to follow any part of the Law for salvation." This is a tremendous stand that Paul is taking.

> **But of these who seemed to be somewhat, (whatsoever they were, it maketh no matter to me: God accepteth no man's person:) for they who seemed to be somewhat in conference added nothing to me [Gal. 2:6].**

Paul says, "We sat down with the apostles (at least *he* did, and I suppose Barnabas and Titus were there also) and communicated the gospel." They said, "Now, Brother Paul, we've been hearing these reports. Tell us what you preach." And Paul told them. Paul finds out that these apostles didn't have anything to add to what he was preaching. He was preaching the grace of God; they were preaching the grace of God. They find they are in full agreement. They all are preaching the same gospel. This is tremendous!

> **But contrariwise, when they saw that the gospel of the uncircumcision was committed unto me, as the gospel of the circumcision was unto Peter [Gal. 2:7].**

Let's understand that there were not two gospels in the sense of Peter's gospel and Paul's gospel. These men were in complete agreement. The gospel of the circumcision and the gospel of the uncircumcision refer to the groups the gospel was going to. The Gentiles were the group that Paul was speaking to. He was called to go to the Gentiles, the uncircumcised. Peter was called to go to his own Jewish brethren who were the circumcised.

> **(For he that wrought effectually in Peter to the apostleship of the circumcision, the same was mighty in me toward the Gentiles:) [Gal. 2:8].**

The proof of the pudding, of course, is always in the eating. What results were they getting? When Peter preached the gospel, quite a few people were saved. When Paul preached the gospel, quite a few people were saved. They were both preaching the same gospel.

Now bringing this principle down to where we live, the real test of any Christian work is not promotion. The real test is the result it gets. God's people should be very sure that they are supporting a ministry that gets results. If it is not producing results, why in the world do you support it?

> **And when James, Cephas, and John, who seemed to be pillars, perceived the grace that was given unto me, they gave to me and Barnabas the right hands of fellowship; that we should go unto the heathen, and they unto the circumcision [Gal. 2:9].**

The apostles accepted Paul's apostleship. "The right hands of fellowship"—fellowship is the Greek *koinonia*, one of the great words of the gospel and the highest expression of a personal relationship. It means sharing the things of Christ.

> **Only they would that we should remember the poor; the same which I also was forward to do [Gal. 2:10].**

Paul came back later with an offering for the poor saints in Jerusalem because that church had been persecuted and was in a sad condition. Because Paul himself before his conversion had led the persecution, he wanted to bring the gift for the Jerusalem church with his own hands.

This was social service. A thing that we fundamentalists are guilty of is a lack of real service in this area. James, in his very practical epistle, says, "If a brother or sister be naked, and destitute of daily food, And one of you say unto them, Depart in peace, be ye warmed and filled; notwithstanding ye give them not those things which are needful to the body; what doth it profit? Even so faith, if it hath not works, is dead, being alone" (James 2:15–17). And the apostles there in Jerusalem said, "Now, Brother Paul, don't forget to help the poor folk." And Paul said, "That was the very thing I was eager to do."

EXPERIENCE OF PAUL IN ANTIOCH WITH PETER

In this personal section of Paul's life we have seen his experience in Arabia with the Lord Jesus Christ, and his experience with the apostles in Jerusalem. Now we see Paul's experience in Antioch with Simon Peter—I love this section.

The church in Antioch was largely a gentile church, although it was a mixture of Jew and Gentile. We will not understand what happened there unless we consider how the early church operated. They had a love feast which was held in connection with the Lord's Supper. Paul has a great deal to say about this subject in 1 Corinthians. The early believers came together for a meal, a love feast, before they celebrated the Lord's Supper. When Gentiles were saved, a problem was raised. In the congregation were Jews who had never eaten anything which had been sacrificed to idols. The Gentiles had been idolaters, and they were accustomed to eating meat that had first been offered to idols. They also ate pork and other animals designated as unclean in the law of Moses. It made no difference to them because they had been reared that way.

What was going to be done to keep from offending the Jewish Christians? Well, in Antioch two tables were established. One was the kosher table; the other was the gentile table. Paul ate at the gentile table. Although he was a Jew, he ate with the Gentiles because he taught that whether you eat meat or you don't eat meat makes no difference—meat will not commend you to God.

When Simon Peter came up to visit Paul in Antioch, it was a new experience for him because, although converted, he had never eaten anything unclean. Remember what Peter told the Lord on the roof in Joppa before he went to the home of Cornelius. He had a vision of heaven opening and a sheet being lowered in which were all kinds of unclean animals. "And there came a voice to him, Rise, Peter; kill, and eat. But Peter said, Not so, Lord; for I have never eaten any thing that is common or unclean. And the voice spake unto him again the second time, What God hath cleansed, that call not thou common" (Acts 10:13–15).

Peter had been a believer for some time when he came to visit Paul in Antioch, but he had still followed the Jewish eating pattern. When Peter came to the church, he found there a gentile table and a kosher table. Now notice Peter's reaction:

> **But when Peter was come to Antioch, I withstood him to the face, because he was to be blamed.**
>
> **For before that certain came from James, he did eat with the Gentiles: but when they were come, he withdrew and separated himself, fearing them which were of the circumcision [Gal. 2:11–12].**

Now this is probably what happened. When the time came to eat, Simon Peter went over to the kosher table, while Paul went over to the gentile table. Peter noticed that there was pork roast on the gentile table. After dinner Peter joined Paul and they went outside for a little walk. Peter said, "I noticed that you ate at the gentile table." "Yes," Paul said. "And I noticed that you ate pork tonight. Is it good? I never have tasted it." "Yes," Paul said, "it's delicious." Then Peter asked, "Do you think it would be all right if I ate over there?" And Paul said, "Well, it is my understanding that we are going to have some nice pork chops in the morning for breakfast. Why don't you try it?" So in the morning when he came to breakfast, he went over to the gentile table, sat down gingerly and rather reluctantly took a pork chop. After he had tasted it, he said to Paul, "It is delicious, isn't it?" Paul said, "Yes. After all, under grace you can either eat it or not eat it. It makes no difference. Meat won't commend you to God." So Simon Peter said, "I'll be here tonight and I understand you are having ham tonight. I want to try that." So at dinner time he starts rushing for the gentile table when he looks over and sees some of the elders from the Jerusalem church who had come to visit also. So Simon Peter went all the way around that gentile table, went over to the kosher table, and sat down like a little whipped puppy. Paul saw him do that, and this is what happened:

> **And the other Jews dissembled likewise with him; insomuch that Barnabas also was carried away with their dissimulation.**
>
> **But when I saw that they walked not uprightly according to the truth of the gospel, I said unto Peter before them all, If thou, being a Jew, livest after the manner of Gentiles, and not as do the Jews, why compellest thou the Gentiles to live as do the Jews? [Gal. 2:13–14].**

It was all right for Peter to eat at either table, kosher or Gentile. But after he had been eating at the gentile table and for fear of the brethren from Jerusalem goes back to the kosher table, he is saying by his action that the gentile table is wrong and the kosher table is right.

Now these brethren from Jerusalem were austere legalists. And under grace that was their privilege. I have no objection to folk today who feel that they should not eat certain meats. But they are also to give me the liberty of eating what I choose to eat. Frankly, I do not eat much pork myself for health reasons. But it is not a religious matter at all. Simon Peter turned from the liberty he had in Christ back to Judaism again.

The nature of Paul's rebuke shows, first of all, the inconsistency of lawkeeping. If it was right for Simon Peter to live as the gentile believers lived, why should he desire the Gentiles to live as the Jews? That is what he was saying when he left the gentile table for the kosher table. If gentile living under grace apart from the Law was good enough for Peter, was it bad for the Gentiles themselves? If Simon Peter was free to live outside the Law, was it not lawful for the Gentiles to do the same?

DOCTRINAL—JUSTIFICATION BY FAITH

This brings us to the doctrinal section of this marvelous epistle, which deals with justification by faith. In this section Paul takes his position as a Jew.

We who are Jews by nature, and not sinners of the Gentiles [Gal. 2:15].

The Jew in that day looked upon the Gentile as a sinner. In fact, Gentile and sinner were synonymous terms. Therefore, the rebuke that Paul gave shows the folly of lawkeeping—how really foolish it is.

Knowing that a man is not justified by the works of the law, but by the faith of Jesus Christ, even we have believed in Jesus Christ, that we might be justified by the faith of Christ, and not by the works of the law: for by the works of the law shall no flesh be justified [Gal. 2:16].

This is a clear-cut and simple statement of justification by faith. Believe me, the legalist has trouble with this verse. I once heard a legalist preach on it, and it was certainly a travesty of interpretation. This verse will upset every legal system there is today. To say that you have to add *anything* to faith in Christ absolutely mutilates the gospel.

Notice what Paul says here. If a Jew had to leave the Law behind—that is, forsake it—in order to be justified by faith, Paul's question is, "Why should the Gentile be brought under the Law?" That was the great argument at the council of Jerusalem in Acts 15: "Should the Gentile be brought under the Law?" Thank God, the answer, guided by the Spirit of God, was that the Gentile was not under the Law for salvation—not for his daily living, as he was called to a much higher plane.

Could the Gentile find justification under the Law when the Jew had already proven that it was impossible? The Jews had had the Law for almost fifteen hundred years and had not been able to keep the Law at all. Why force the Gentile under that which had not saved even one Israelite? Gentile believers were already justified by grace. It would be folly for the Gentiles to turn from grace to the Law which had been unable to justify the Jew.

"Knowing that a man." Now let's pick this verse apart. This is something you can *know*—you can know whether you are saved or not. What kind of "man" is this verse speaking about? *Anthrōpos* is the Greek word, a generic term meaning "mankind." It speaks of the solidarity of the race, the common humanity that we all have. This breaks the social barrier of color. It breaks the barrier of race. It breaks the social barrier. All men are on one level before the Cross, and that level happens to be "sinner." You are a sinner. I am a sinner. I don't care who you are, you are a sinner in God's sight.

"Knowing that a man is not justified by the works of the law"—the word *the* is not in the original; so it should read "not justified by works of law." This includes the Mosaic system, and it includes any legal system. This is what I mean: if you say that you have to join a certain church, or that you have to have a certain experience, or that you have to be baptized to be saved, you are contradicting this verse. "Knowing that a man is not justified by works of law"—any law. Paul embraces the whole legal system that is found in every religion. This makes Christianity different from every religion on topside of the earth. Every religion that I know anything about—and I have studied many of the cults and religions of this world—instruct us to *do* something. Christianity is different. It tells us that we are justified by faith; that is, faith is an accomplished act and fact for you. Every other religion says *do*. Christianity says *done*. The great transaction is *done*, and we are asked to believe it.

Let me call your attention to an important verse in 1 Corinthians: "Wherefore I give you to understand, that no man speaking by the Spirit of God calleth Jesus accursed: and that no man can say that Jesus is the Lord, but by the Holy Ghost" (1 Cor. 12:3). Now the question for you and me is: how can we call Jesus accursed? If you say to me, "McGee, when you came to Christ and accepted Him as your Savior, you didn't get all that was coming to you. The Holy Spirit can give you something that you didn't get in Christ, and you ought to seek that today?" My friend, to do that depreciates the work of the Lord Jesus on the cross when He came to this earth to die for you and work out a salvation so perfect that when He went back to heaven He sat down at the right hand of God (see Heb. 1:3). He sat down because there was nothing else to be done. If there had been anything else, He would have done it before He sat down. When you say that He didn't do it all for me, you are saying that Jesus is accursed. And you can't say that by the Holy Spirit of God. That is, you are not giving me the word of the Holy Spirit. Jesus said, "Howbeit when he, the Spirit of truth, is come, he will guide you into all truth: for he shall not speak of himself; but whatsoever he shall hear, that shall he speak: and he will shew you things to come. He shall glorify me: for he shall receive of mine, and shall shew it unto you" (John 16:13–14). My friend, when you came to Christ, He gave you everything you will need in this life. Christ is the One who administers all the gifts. The Holy Spirit is the One who gives them, but He is working down here under the supervision of the second Person of the Godhead. The Lord Jesus Christ is the Head of the church. My friend, we have everything in Him. He is the Alpha and the Omega. He is the Amen— and when you say "amen," you are through, my friend. Christ did it all.

This verse is so clear it is impossible to misunderstand it. "Knowing that a man (any human being—man or woman, black or white, rich or poor, Roman, American, Chinese) is not justified by the works of the law, but by the faith of Jesus Christ." It is not faith plus something; it is faith plus *nothing*.

The verse continues: "even we have believed in Jesus Christ, that we might be justified by the faith of Christ." Who does Paul mean by "we"? He includes himself, meaning we Israelites. He is saying that he and his fellow Jews had to leave the Law, come to Christ, and trust Him in order to be justified by the faith of Christ rather than by the works of law.

The conclusion of this verse is so clear I feel that anybody can understand it: "for by the works of the law shall *no flesh be justified*." Let's not depreciate the work of the Lord Jesus by saying that we didn't get everything from Him. I was a hell-doomed sinner. I trusted Him as my Savior, and I received a perfect salvation from Him.

Now the next verse, I am frank to say, is a little more difficult to understand.

> **But if, while we seek to be justified by Christ, we ourselves also are found sinners, is therefore Christ the minister of sin? God forbid [Gal. 2:17].**

The word *justified* is the Greek *dikaioō*, which means "to declare a person right," or "to make him right." We are declared to be right by our faith in Jesus Christ. It means that a sinner who is guilty before God, who is under condemnation and judgment, is declared to be right with God on the basis of his faith in the redemption which we have in Christ. It is not only forgiveness of sins, which is subtraction; it is the addition of the righteousness of Christ. He is declared righteous. The righteousness I have is not my own righteousness, because *my* righteousness is not acceptable; but I have a perfect righteousness which is Christ.

The sense of this verse seems to be this: Since the Jew had to forsake the Law in order to be justified by Christ and therefore take his place as a sinner, is Christ the One who makes him a sinner? Paul's answer is, "Of course not." The Jew, like the Gentile, was a sinner by nature. He could not be justified by the Law, as he demonstrated. This same thought was given by Peter in his address before the great council at Jerusalem: "Now therefore why tempt ye God, to put a yoke upon the neck of the disciples, which neither our fathers nor we were able to bear? But we believe that through the grace of the Lord Jesus Christ we shall be saved, even as they" (Acts 15:10–11). You see, Peter and Paul were in agreement on the doctrine of justification by faith.

> **For if I build again the things which I destroyed, I make myself a transgressor [Gal. 2:18].**

In other words, Paul is saying, "If I go back under law, I make myself a transgressor."

However he is free from the Law. How did he become free from the Law?

> **For I through the law am dead to the law, that I might live unto God [Gal. 2:19].**

Paul is saying, "When Christ died, He died for me. He died in my stead because the Law had condemned me." You see, the Law was a ministration of condemnation; a ministration of death is what Paul calls it in 2 Corinthians 3:7. It condemns me. Even under the legal system God would have had to destroy the nation Israel. But He gave the sacrificial system—five sacrifices—all of them pointing to Christ. God, by His marvelous grace, was able to save. Therefore the mercy seat was a throne of grace where a nation could find forgiveness of sins. The Law, therefore, condemned me. The Law has accused man. We stand guilty before the Law. So the Law actually is responsible for Jesus' dying for us. The Law condemned us—said we had to die. All right now, if I am dead to the Law, then I am no longer responsible to the Law. The Law has already killed me. It has executed me, and I am dead—dead to the Law. Therefore, the Law could not do for me what Christ has done for me. He not only took my place and died for me, but He also did something else. He was able to give me life. He came back from the dead. You see, the Law arrested, condemned, sentenced, and slew us—that is all the Law could do for us. If you want to come by the Law route, you'll get death. Only Christ can give you life. And, after all, life is what we need today.

> **I am crucified with Christ: nevertheless I live; yet not I, but Christ liveth in me: and the life which I now live in the flesh I live by the faith of the Son of God, who loved me, and gave himself for me [Gal. 2:20].**

This verse states a fact which is true of every believer. We are not to *seek* to be crucified with Christ. I have been to many young people's conferences, and I do not think I am exaggerating when I say that I have seen thousands of young people accept Christ. I have also heard many of those young people at testimony meetings quote verse 20 as they put a faggot on the fire. They did not know any more about what this verse means than does a goat grazing on a hillside.

There are many people today who talk about wanting to live the "crucified" life. That is not what Paul is talking about in this verse. We are not to seek to be crucified with Christ. We have already been crucified with Him. The principle of living is not by the Law which has slain us because it found us guilty. Now we are to live by faith. Faith in what? Faith in the Son of God. You see, friend, the death of

Christ upon the cross was not only penal (that is, paying the penalty for our sins), but it was substitutionary also. He was not only the *sacrifice* for sin; He was the *substitute* for all who believe.

Paul declares, therefore, that under the Law he was tried, found guilty, was condemned, and in the person of his Substitute he was slain. When did that take place? It took place when Christ was crucified. Paul was crucified with Christ. But "nevertheless I live." How do I live? In Christ. He is alive today at God's right hand. We are told that we have been put in Christ. You cannot improve on that. That ought to get rid of the foolish notion that we can crucify ourselves.

When I was a pastor in Los Angeles, a young man came to me after a service and asked, "Dr. McGee, are you living the crucified life?" I think I rather startled the boy when I replied, "No, I am not." Then I asked him, "Are you?" He hesitated for a moment and then said, "Well, I am trying to." Then I told him, "That is not the question you asked me. You wanted to know if I am living the crucified life. I told you no. Now you tell me yes or no about your life. Are you living the crucified life?" Once again he replied, "I am trying to." I said to him, "You are either living it, or you are not living it. The fact of the matter is you cannot live it." "Oh," he said, "why can't I?" So I pointed out to him that there is something interesting to note about crucifixion. You can commit suicide in many different ways. You can hang yourself, shoot yourself, take poison, jump off a high building, or jump in front of a truck. There are many ways to end your life, but you cannot crucify yourself. When you nail one hand to the cross, who is going to nail your other hand to the cross? You cannot do it yourself. You must understand what Paul is talking about when he says, "I am crucified with Christ." Paul was crucified with Christ when Christ died. Christ died a substitutionary death. He died for Paul. He died for you. He died for me.

In Romans 6 we are told that we have been buried with Christ by baptism, by identification. We have been raised with Him in newness of life, and now we are joined to the living Christ. Paul says that we do not know Him any more after the flesh. He is not the Man of Galilee walking around the Sea of Galilee. I walked about in that area some time ago and did not see Him; He is not there today. He is at God's right hand. He is the glorified Christ.

Paul is saying, "I am crucified with Christ: nevertheless I live." You see, the Law executed us. The Law could not give us life. Who gave us life? "I am crucified with Christ: nevertheless *I live*." How do you live? "Yet not I, but *Christ liveth in me*." My friend, that is the important thing. He died for me down here that I might live in Him up yonder and that He might live in me down here. "And the life," Paul says, "which I now live in the flesh I live by the faith of the Son of God." What kind of life is this? It is a life of faith—saved by faith, live by faith, walk by faith. This is what it means to walk in the Spirit.

"I live by the faith of the Son of God"—how tender this is—"who *loved* me, and gave himself for me." Christ loved me, but He could not *love* me into heaven. He had to *give* Himself for me. The gift of God is eternal life in Christ Jesus. You can receive a gift only by faith. This applies to any gift, for that matter. You have to believe that the giver who holds out the gift to you is sincere. You must believe that he is telling the truth when he holds it out to you and says, "It is yours." You have to reach out in faith and take it before it belongs to you. God offers you the gift of eternal life in Christ Jesus.

The content of this verse leads me to believe that Paul was present at the crucifixion of Christ. Paul was a Pharisee, and they were the ones who led in the Crucifixion. Paul was a leader in the persecution of the church. He was also one who hated the Lord Jesus Christ. He probably was attending school in Jerusalem, in the school of Gamaliel, at the time of the Crucifixion. I cannot believe this zealous young man would stay home on the day Jesus was crucified. The Scriptures tell us that the Pharisees ridiculed Jesus. They told Him to come down from the cross. Then they sat down and watched Him die—you cannot sink any lower than that. I believe Paul was there that day.

Now after Paul came to know the glorified Christ, the One who died down here, the One who rose again and is at God's right hand, Paul could remember that day and say, "While I was there ridiculing Him, shooting out the lip at Him, expressing my hatred for Him, He loved me and He gave Himself for me!" He gave Himself—the supreme sacrifice. Paul called himself the chief of sinners, which was not hyperbole or an oratorical gesture. It was an actual fact; he was the chief of sinners.

My friend, you can tread underfoot the precious blood of Christ by ignoring Him, turning away from Him, or turning against Him as Paul did. But it was for that crowd that Jesus prayed, ". . . Father, forgive them; for they know not what they do . . ." (Luke 23:34). Even if you hate Him, He was loving you and giving Himself for you.

I do not frustrate the grace of God: for if righteousness come by the law, then Christ is dead in vain [Gal. 2:21].

The main thought in this verse is simply that if there had been any other way to save sinners, then God would have used that method. If a law or a religion could have been given that would save sinners, God would have given it. The only way that an infinite God could save you and me was to send His Son to die. He was willing to make the supreme sacrifice.

CHAPTER 3

THEME: Justification by faith; experience of the Galatians; illustration of Abraham

EXPERIENCE OF THE GALATIANS

Paul now goes back to the experience of the Galatians. How were they saved? Were they saved by law or were they saved by faith in Jesus Christ? I personally believe in experience. I had a Methodist background as a boy. I went down to a penitent altar underneath a brush arbor in back of an unpainted Methodist church in southern Oklahoma. I was just a little fellow and I knelt there with an open heart. I believe in experience, and when we come to chapter 4 we will deal further with the subject of experience.

> **O foolish Galatians, who hath bewitched you, that ye should not obey the truth, before whose eyes Jesus Christ hath been evidently set forth, crucified among you? [Gal. 3:1].**

"O foolish Galatians"—senseless Galatians. The Greek word is *anoetoi* from the root word *nous*, meaning "mind." He is saying, "You're not using your mind—you're not using your *nous*."

"Who hath bewitched you?" Let me translate that in good old Americano: What's gotten into you? "Before whose eyes Jesus Christ hath been evidently set forth"—"set forth" is literally *placarded* or *painted*. I am not sure that Paul actually drew pictures for the Galatians, but I am sure that he painted word pictures for them. I used to show a great many slides when I was a pastor. It is a marvelous way of teaching the Word of God. For example, I would not attempt to teach the tabernacle without using slides. Now that is the way you "set forth" a teaching, and that is the word Paul uses. "Set forth, crucified among you"—it was His death on the cross that made possible your salvation!

This only would I learn of you, Received ye the Spirit by the works of the law, or by the hearing of faith? [Gal. 3:2].

Now we need to be very careful here. The gospel is true irrespective of experience. What experience does is corroborate the gospel. There are many people today who reason from experience to truth. I personally believe that the Word of God reasons from truth to experience. Experience is not be discounted, but it must be tested by truth.

Everyone has different experiences. I heard one of the founders of a cult tell about her experience. Then I heard another woman tell about her experience—and they are entirely different. Which person am I going to follow? To tell the truth, I am not going to follow either one of them.

One time a man got up in a meeting and read a passage of Scripture. He said, "Because there is a difference of opinion concerning the interpretation of this passage, and we don't want any controversy, let me tell you about my experience." Well, his experience was as far removed from what that Scripture said as anything could possibly be. He was basing truth on his experience. You simply cannot do that. Experience must corroborate the gospel.

"Received ye the Spirit by the works of the law, or by the hearing of faith?" What does Paul mean by the *hearing* of faith? Does he mean the ear, the organ of hearing, or the receiving of the message, or the message itself? I think he means the whole process. You have to hear something before you can be saved, because the gospel is something God has done for you, and you need to know about it.

In this section Paul is raising several questions. He tells these folk to look back to what had happened to them and asks six questions that have to do with their experience.

This is his first question: "Received ye the Spirit by the works of the law, or by the hearing of faith?" Nowhere—not even in the Old Testament—did anyone ever receive the Holy Spirit by the works of the Law. He is received by the hearing of faith. The Galatians never received the Spirit by the Law. The Holy Spirit is evidence of conversion. Scripture tells us, "But ye are not in the flesh, but in the Spirit, if so be that the Spirit of God dwell in you. Now if any man have not the Spirit of Christ, he is none of his" (Rom. 8:9). "In whom ye also trusted, after that ye heard the word of truth, the gospel of your salvation: in whom also after that ye believed, ye were sealed with that holy Spirit of promise" (Eph. 1:13).

Now here is the second question:

Are ye so foolish? having begun in the Spirit, are ye now made perfect by the flesh? [Gal. 3:3].

What Paul is asking is this: "If the Holy Spirit is the One who converted you, brought you to Christ, and now you are indwelt by the Spirit of God, are you going to turn back to the Law (which was given to control the flesh) and think you are going to live on a high plane?"

Have ye suffered so many things in vain? if it be yet in vain [Gal. 3:4].

Paul asked the Galatians, "Are you going to let all of the things you have suffered come to naught?" He reminded them that they had paid a price for receiving the gospel. Was it all going to be in vain, without a purpose?

Now he raises this question:

He therefore that ministereth to you the Spirit, and worketh miracles among you, doeth he it by the works of the law, or by the hearing of faith? [Gal. 3:5].

Paul refers to the ministry that he has led among them. You will recall that his apostleship was attacked by the Judaizers. They said that he was a Johnny-come-lately apostle—not one of the original Twelve. He was not with Christ during His ministry but came along later. Paul reminded the Galatians that he was the one who had come into their country, preached the Word of God to them, and performed miracles among them. He did not do it by the works of the Law—Paul would be very careful to say that. He preached the Lord Jesus Christ as the One who died for them, was raised again, and in whom they placed their trust. When they did that, a miraculous thing took place. They were regenerated. Paul had the evidence that he was an apostle. In that day sings were given to the apostles. As I understand it, the apostles had practically all the gifts mentioned in Scripture; they certainly had all the sign gifts. Paul could perform miracles. He could heal the sick. He could raise the dead. Simon Peter, one of the original Twelve, could do that also. To do this was the mark of an apostle in that day.

Now the apostles have given us the Word of God. We have a faith that is built upon Jesus Christ as the chief cornerstone, and a faith built upon the foundation which was laid by the apostles and prophets. That which gave credence to the truth of their message was their ability to perform miracles. They had the sign gifts. (After they had given us the Word of God, the sign gifts disappeared. In fact, I think they disappeared with the apostles.) The important thing for us to note here is that Paul came to the Galatians not as a Pharisee preaching the Law, but as an apostle preaching Jesus Christ. That was something these people had experienced, and Paul rested upon that.

In summary, we have seen that justification by faith was the experience of the Galatians. That is why he asked them, "What has gotten into you?" He mentions the Holy Spirit three times in this section. He reminds them that they did not receive the Spirit by the Law. The Holy Spirit is evidence of conversion. It is important to see that the gospel is true irrespective of the experience of the Galatians or anyone else. The gospel is objective; it deals with what the Lord Jesus Christ did for us. Experience will corroborate the gospel, and that is what Paul is demonstrating in this section. The gospel is sufficient—experience confirms this.

ILLUSTRATION OF ABRAHAM

This section of justification by faith using Abraham as an illustration looms large in this epistle. Then follows an allegory of Hagar and Sarai, which takes us through the rest of chapter 4. So now we come to the heart of this book, the high water mark, where Abraham will be the illustration.

Even as Abraham believed God, and it was accounted to him for righteousness [Gal. 3:6].

This verse is a quote from Genesis 15:6 concerning Abraham, "And he believed in the LORD; and he counted it to him for righteousness." This verse is also quoted in Romans 4:3. The illustration comes from the early part of the life of Abraham, his life of faith. Abraham is the great illustration of justification by faith. Paul uses him as an example in both the Roman and Galatian epistles. It cannot be said that Abraham was justified by the Law because the Mosaic Law was not given until four hundred years after Abraham. Neither can it be said that he was justified *before* God gave him the commandment of circumcision. Circumcision was the badge and evidence of Abraham's faith, just as baptism is the badge and evidence of a believer's faith today. Neither circumcision nor baptism can save. In fact, they make no contribution to salvation. They are simply outward evidences of an inward work.

The incident referred to is in Genesis 15. After Abraham encountered the kings of the East in his rescue of his nephew Lot, he refused to accept any booty from the kings of Sodom and Gomorrah. God appeared to Abraham to assure him that he had done right in turning down the booty, saying, "I am your shield, and your exceeding great reward." Abraham was a practical sort of individual, and he began talking to the Lord rather straight—and I feel that the Lord wants us to do that, friend. He said, "I don't have a son, and You told me I would." The Lord said, "I'm glad you brought that up, Abraham, I've been wanting to tell you something." God had already told him that his seed would be as numberless as the sand on the seashore. Now God takes him by the hand and tells him to look toward the heavens. It must have been night time. I am told in that section of the world one can see about five thousand stars with the naked eye. With a sixteen inch telescope you would see fifty thousand stars, and I don't know what you would see with a hundred inch or two hundred inch telescope. Be that as it may, I don't think any telescope could give you the exact number of stars which could be seen at that time. In effect, God said to Abraham, "You can't count the stars, and neither can you count your offspring." Do you know what Abraham's response was? "And he believed in the LORD;

and he counted it to him for righteousness" (Gen. 15:6). In the original it is very expressive. Literally it means that Abraham said "amen" to the Lord. God said, "I'm going to do it." And Abraham said, "Amen."

Does this have an application for your life and mine? It certainly does. God says to you and me, "I gave My Son to die for you. If you believe on Him you won't perish. You will have everlasting life." Will you say "amen" to that? Will you believe God? Will you accept His son? If you do, you are justified by faith. This is what Abraham did. He believed God, and at that moment God declared him righteous. Because of his works? No! His works were imperfect. He didn't have perfection to offer to God. (Paul will develop this thought a little later on.) Although Abraham did not have perfection at that time, afterwards he did because his faith was counted for righteousness. That is the doctrine of justification. Abraham stands justified before God.

Next Abraham said to the Lord, "Would you mind putting what you have told me in writing?" Perhaps you are saying, "I have read the Book of Genesis, and I don't remember anything like that." Well, it's here in Genesis 15. Now notice: "And he said unto him, I am the LORD that brought thee out of Ur of the Chaldees, to give thee this land to inherit it" (Gen. 15:7). Listen to Abraham's response. He is talking back to the Lord—he's not one of these superpious saints. "And he said, Lord GOD, whereby shall I know that I shall inherit it?" (Gen. 15:8). In other words, put it in writing. God said to Abraham, "Meet me down at the courthouse and I will put it in writing." Now somebody says, "Wait a minute. It doesn't say that." But it does, friend. "And he said unto him, Take me an heifer of three years old, and a she goat of three years old, and a ram of three years old, and a turtledove, and a young pigeon" (Gen. 15:9). That is the way they made contracts in that day. (Jeremiah also tells about making a contract in this way in Jeremiah 34:18). You see, when a contract was made in that day, one man agreed to do something, and the other man agreed to do something in turn. They cut a sacrifice into two parts and put half on one side and half on the other side, then they would join hands and walk between the two halves. That sealed the contract. It was the same as going before a notary at the courthouse.

So Abraham prepared the sacrifices and waited—he waited all day. Fowls came down upon the carcasses and Abraham drove them away. God was late meeting Abraham; He did not get there until sundown. "And when the sun was going down, a deep sleep fell upon Abram; and, lo, an horror of great darkness fell upon him" (Gen. 15:12). Just as he is about to sign the contract, God puts Abraham in to a deep sleep. The reason for this is that Abraham is not to walk with God through the two halves—Abraham is not to promise anything. God is doing the promising. "And it came to pass, that, when the sun went down, and it was dark, behold a smoking furnace, and a burning lamp that passed between those pieces" (Gen. 15:17). You see, God passed through between those two halves alone because God made the covenant. And Abraham's part was only to believe God. If the covenant depended on Abraham's faithfulness—perhaps on his saying his prayers every night—he might miss one night, and then the promise would be no good. So God was the One who did all the promising, and the covenant depended on God's faithfulness.

Friend, over nineteen hundred years ago Jesus Christ went to the cross to pay for your sins and mine. God is not asking you to say your prayers or be a nice little Sunday school boy to be saved. He is asking you to trust His Son who died for you. He makes the contract. He is the One who makes the promise, the covenant, and He will save you. That is the new contract, friend. The old covenant He made with Abraham. Abraham believed God. He said, "amen," to God. Abraham believed, and it was accounted to him for righteousness. God is still asking us to believe Him. Put your trust in Christ and you will be saved. What a glorious picture we have here.

Know ye therefore that they which are of faith, the same are the children of Abraham [Gal. 3:7].

God did this for Abraham before the Law was ever given. God did not make the covenant with him because of Abraham's good works. He told Abraham, "I'll do this for you if you believe Me." Abraham said, "I believe You."

God wants your faith to rest on a solid foundation. But, my friend, if you come to God, you must come to Him by faith. He has come to the door of your heart. He cannot come any farther. He will not break down the door. He will knock and say, "Behold, I stand at the door, and knock: if any man hear my voice, and open the door, I will come in to him, and will sup with him, and he with me" (Rev. 3:20). Only you can open the door by faith, my friend. When you and I trust Christ as Savior, we are saved the same way that Abraham was saved—by faith.

And the scripture, foreseeing that God would justify the heathen through faith, preached before the gospel unto Abraham, saying, In thee shall all nations be blessed [Gal. 3:8].

"And the scripture, foreseeing that God would justify the heathen through faith, preached before the gospel unto Abraham." If faith without works was sufficient for Abraham, why should we desire something different? And as the blessing was not for Abraham's law-works, but for his faith, why should we turn from faith to law-works?

"God . . . preached . . . the gospel unto Abraham." When did He do that? Well, the first illustration Paul gave us was at the beginning of Abraham's life of faith. Now Paul refers to an incident near the end of Abraham's life of faith recorded in Genesis 22. It was after Abraham had offered Isaac upon the altar. I say he offered him because he was just within a hair's breadth of offering him when God stopped him. God considered that Abraham had actually done it. He demonstrated that he had faith in God, believing that God could raise Isaac from the dead (see Heb. 11:19). Now notice God's response to Abraham's act of faith: "And the angel of the LORD called unto Abraham out of heaven the second time, and said, By myself have I sworn, saith the LORD, for because thou hast done this thing, and hast not withheld thy son, thine only son: that in blessing I will bless thee, and in multiplying I will multiply thy seed as the stars of the heaven, and as the sand which is upon the sea shore; and thy seed shall possess the gate of his enemies; and in thy seed shall all the nations of the earth be blessed; because thou hast obeyed my voice" (Gen. 22:15–18). Apparently at this time God preached the gospel to Abraham, because the offering of

Isaac is one of the finest pictures of the offering of Christ. Although God spared Abraham's son, God did not spare His own Son but delivered Him up for us all.

The important thing that Paul wants us to see in Abraham's life is that he obeyed the voice of God. Abraham was willing to offer his son when God commanded it, and when God said stop, he stopped. He obeyed the voice of God. He demonstrated by his action that he had faith in God. Again he believed God and He counted it to him for righteousness.

Some people are troubled because they feel that there is a contradiction in Scripture between what Paul says about Abraham and what James says about him. Paul says that Abraham was justified by faith. James says, "But wilt thou know, O vain man, that faith without works is dead? Was not Abraham our father justified by works, when he had offered Isaac his son upon the altar?" (James 2:20–21). However, James goes on to say, "Seest thou how faith wrought with his works, and by works was faith made perfect?" (James 2:22). John Calvin said it like this: "Faith alone saves, but the faith that saves is not alone." In other words, saving faith is a dynamic, vital faith that leads to works. I hope you understand that James is not talking about the works of law. James is talking about the works of faith. Faith produces works. This idea of saying that works will save you is putting the cart before the horse—in fact, some men put the horse in the cart!

It is important to see that faith leads to works, as it did in the life of Abraham. God sees our hearts. He knows whether or not we have trusted Christ as Savior. He knows whether or not we are genuine. Church member, why not be genuine? You can fool the people in the church, and you can fool your neighbors, and you can put up a pious front. But why not be *real* and have a lot of fun at the same time? You don't have to pretend. You can be real and trust Christ as your Savior. And a living, dynamic faith will produce works.

A careful reading of the passage in James 2 reveals that James used the history of Abraham to show that faith without works is dead—it is the last of Abraham's history because this is the last time God appeared to him. It is not the portion of Scripture to which Paul refers in Galatians where he says that Abraham was justified by faith. Paul says that faith alone is sufficient and proves his point from Abraham's history as recorded in the fifteenth chapter of Genesis. James says that faith without works is dead and proves it by referring to Abraham's history as found in the twenty-second chapter of Genesis. If Abraham had welshed in Genesis 22 and had said to God, "Wait a minute, I really do not believe what You say. I have been putting on an act all of these years," then it would have been obvious that Abraham's faith was a pseudofaith. But God knew back in Genesis 15 that Abraham had a genuine faith.

The works that James speaks about are not works of law at all. The Law had not been given during Abraham's day. We need to recognize that. James 2:23 says, "And the scripture was fulfilled which saith, Abraham believed God, and it was imputed unto him for righteousness: and he was called the Friend of God." James, at the beginning of this verse, is going back to the reference that Paul gives at first concerning the beginning of Abraham's life of faith. Then Paul says that the gospel was preached to Abraham at the end of his life when God made this promise to him.

There is no contradiction when you examine passages like the ones written by Paul and James. They are saying the same thing. One is looking at faith at the beginning. The other is looking at faith at the end. One is looking at the *root* of faith. The other is looking at the *fruit* of faith. The root of faith is "faith alone saves you," but that saving faith will produce works.

So then they which be of faith are blessed with faithful Abraham [Gal. 3:9].

The word *faithful* in this verse is "believing"—believing Abraham. God saves the sinner today on the same basis that He saved Abraham. God asks *faith* of the sinner. God asked Abraham to believe that He would do certain things for him. God asks you and me to believe that He already has done certain things for us in giving His Son, Jesus Christ to die for us. Faith is the modus operandi by which man is saved today.

For as many as are of the works of the law are under the curse: for it is written, Cursed is every one that continueth not in all things which are written in the book of the law to do them [Gal. 3:10].

The important word here is "continueth." I am willing to grant that maybe there was a day in your life when you felt very good, when you were on top of the world and singing, "Everything's coming up daisies." On that day you walked with the Lord and did not stub your toe. Then you say, "Well, because I did that, God saved me." But notice what this verse says, "Cursed is every one that *continueth* not in all things which are written in the book of the law." How about that? Do you keep the law day and night, twenty-four hours every day, seven days a week, fifty-two weeks out of the year in thought, word, and deed? If you are a human being, somewhere along the line you let down. You are not walking on top of the world all the time. My friend, when you let down, the law can only condemn you.

I know a fine preacher who is always going around saying, "Hallelujah, praise the Lord." Someone asked his wife if he was like that all the time. She said, "No, he has his bad days." We all have bad days, don't we?

If you are going to put yourself under the law, my friend, and you have a good day, you are not going to be rewarded for it. Suppose I had kept all of the laws of Pasadena, which is my home city, for twenty years. Then I wait at my house for the officials of Pasadena to come and present me with a medal for keeping those laws. Let me tell you, they do not give medals for keeping the law in Pasadena. If I had kept every law for twenty years and then stole something or broke a speeding law, I would be arrested. You see, the law does not reward you. It does not give you life. The law penalizes you.

Faith, my friend, gives you something. It gives you life.

But that no man is justified by the law in the sight of God, it is evident: for, The just shall live by faith [Gal. 3:11].

Even the Old Testament taught that man was saved by faith. It does not say that anyone was saved by keeping the law. If you find that somebody living back under the law was saved by keeping the law, let me know. I have never read of anyone who was saved by keeping the Mosaic Law. As you know, the heart of the Mosaic system was the sacrificial system. Moses rejoiced that God could extend mercy and grace to people even under the law—that is the reason his face shone as it did. In Habakkuk 2:4 it says that ". . . the just shall live by his faith."

> **And the law is not of faith: but, The man that doeth them shall live in them [Gal. 3:12].**

This also is an important verse. Faith and law are contrary principles for salvation and also for living. One cancels out the other. They are diametrically opposed to each other. If you are going to live by the Law, then you cannot be saved by faith. You cannot combine them. They are contrary.

Let me illustrate this. Our daughter came to visit us while we were in Florida, and we wanted to return to California by train. That was the time when passenger trains were being phased out. We tried to get a train route to California without going through Chicago—both of us wanted to avoid Chicago. Well, it seemed as though we would have to go halfway around the world to go from Florida to California; so we had to come back by plane. When we got the tickets, I said, "Wouldn't it be nice if we could go by train and plane at the same time—sit in the plane and put our feet down in the train!" (I would feel much safer with my feet in the train, I assure you). But that's absurd. If we go by plane, we go by plane; if we go by train, we go by train. They have made no arrangements for passengers to sit in a plane and put their feet down in a train. My friend, neither has God any arrangement for you to be saved by faith and by law. You have to choose one or the other. If you want to go by law, then you can try it—but I'll warn you that God has already said you won't make it. "The law is not of faith: but, The man that doeth them shall live in them."

> **Christ hath redeemed us from the curse of the law, being made a curse for us: for it is written, Cursed is every one that hangeth on a tree [Gal. 3:13].**

"Christ hath redeemed us from the curse of the law"—the Mosaic Law *condemned* us. It is like the illustration I gave regarding keeping the civil laws in my hometown. I am not rewarded for keeping those laws, and if I break one I am condemned. Christ has redeemed us from the penalty of the Mosaic Law. How did He do it? By "being made a curse for us." Christ bore that penalty.

"For it is written, Cursed is every one that hangeth on a tree." This is a quotation from the Old Testament, as we shall see, and is a remarkable passage of Scripture for several reasons. One reason is that the children of Israel did not use hanging on a tree as a method of public execution. Instead they used stoning. When my wife went with me to the land of Israel, she noticed something that I had not thought of. She said, "I have often wondered why they used stoning as a means of execution. Now I know. Anywhere you turn in this land there are plenty of stones." Capital punishment in Israel was by stoning, not hanging. However, when a reprehensible crime had been committed, this was the procedure: "And if a man have committed a sin worthy of death, and he be to be put to death, and thou hang him on a tree: His body shall not remain all night upon the tree, but thou shalt in any wise bury him that day; (for he that is hanged is accursed of God;) that thy land be not defiled, which the LORD thy God giveth thee for an inheritance" (Deut. 21:22–23). That is, if he had committed an awful crime and had bene stoned to death, his body could be strung up on a tree that it might be a spectacle. But it was not to be left there overnight. The reason He gives is this: he is accursed of God— "that thy land be not defiled, which the LORD thy God giveth thee for an inheritance."

Christ was "made a curse for us." The question is: When did Christ become a curse? Did He become a curse in His incarnation? Oh, no. When He was born He was called ". . . that holy thing . . ." (Luke 1:35). Did He become a curse during those silent years of which we have so little record? No, it says that He advanced ". . . in favour with God and man" (Luke 2:52). Did He become a curse during his ministry? Oh, no. It was during His ministry that the Father said, ". . . This is my beloved Son, in whom I am well pleased" (Matt. 3:17). Then He must have become a curse while He was on the cross. Yes, but not during the first three hours on the cross, because when He offered up Himself, He was without blemish. It was during those last three hours on the cross that He was made a curse for us. It was then that it pleased the Lord to bruise Him and put Him to grief. He made His soul an offering for sin (see Isa. 53:10).

"Cursed is everyone that hangeth on a tree." The Greek word for "tree" is *xulon*, meaning "wood, timber, or tree." Christ was hanged on a tree. What a contrast we have here. He went to that cross, which was to Him a tree of death, in order that He might make it for you and me a tree of life!

> **That the blessing of Abraham might come on the Gentiles through Jesus Christ; that we might receive the promise of the Spirit through faith [Gal. 3:14].**

Israel had the Law for fifteen hundred years and failed to live by it. At the council of Jerusalem, in Acts 15, Peter said in effect, "We and our fathers were not able to keep the law. Why do we want to put the Gentiles under it? If we could not keep it, they won't be able to keep it either." Christ took our place that we might receive what the Law could never do. The Spirit is the peculiar gift in this age of grace.

> **Brethren, I speak after the manner of men; Though it be but a man's covenant, yet if it be confirmed, no man disannulleth, or addeth thereto [Gal. 3:15].**

Suppose you make a contract with a man to pay him one hundred dollars. Then about a year later you decide you will pay him only fifty dollars. You go to him and say, "Here is the fifty dollars I owe you." The man says, "Wait a minute, you agreed to pay me one hundred dollars." You say, "Well, I've changed that." He says, "Oh, no, you don't! You can't change your contract after it has been made."

> **Now to Abraham and his seed were the promises made. He saith not, And to seeds, as of many; but as of one, And to thy seed, which is Christ [Gal. 3:16].**

God called Abraham and promised to make him a blessing to the world. He made him a blessing to the world through Jesus Christ, a descendant of Abraham. Christ is the One who brought salvation to the world.

The word *seed* refers specifically to Christ (see Gen. 22:18). Christ said, "Your father Abraham rejoiced to see my day: and he saw it, and was glad" (John 8:56).

And this I say, that the covenant, that was confirmed before of God in Christ, the law, which was four hundred and thirty years after, cannot disannul, that it should make the promise of none effect [Gal. 3:17].

God made a promise, a covenant, with Abraham. When the Law came along "four hundred and thirty years" later, it didn't change anything as far as the promises made to Abraham were concerned. Actually, God never goes back on His promises. God promised Abraham, "I am going to give you this land. I am going to give you a son and a people that will be as numberless as the sand on the seashore." God fulfilled that promise and brought from Abraham the nation of Israel—and several other nations—but the promises were given through Isaac whose line led to the Lord Jesus Christ, the "Seed" of verse 16. God also promised Abraham that He would make him a blessing to all people. The only blessing, my friend, in this world today is in Christ. You may not get a very good deal from your neighbor or from your business or from your church. I don't think the world is prepared to give you a good deal. But the Lord Jesus Christ has been given to you—that is a good deal! In fact it is the supreme gift which God has made. It is a fulfillment of God's promise that He would save those who would trust Christ.

For if the inheritance be of the law, it is no more of promise: but God gave it to Abraham by promise [Gal. 3:18].

The promise concerning Christ was made before the Mosaic Law was given, and that promise holds as good as though there had been no law given, my friend. The promise was made irrespective of the Law.

The question arises: Why was the Law given, of what value is it? Now don't think that Paul is playing down the Law. Rather, he is trying to help the people understand the *purpose* of the Law. He shows the Law in all of its majesty, in its fullness, and in its perfection. But he shows that this very perfection the Law reveals is the reason it creates a hurdle which you and I cannot get over in order to be accepted of God.

Now listen to Paul as he talks about the purpose of the Law.

Wherefore then serveth the law? It was added because of transgressions, till the seed should come to whom the promise was made; and it was ordained by angels in the hand of a mediator [Gal. 3:19].

The question is: Wherefore then serveth the Law? He is giving a purpose sentence—what was the purpose of the Law? Paul says it was something that was added. It was added because—or better still—for the sake of transgressions.

"Till the seed should come"—that little word *till* is an important time word. It means the Law was temporary. The Law was given for the interval between the time of Moses until the time of Christ. "For the law was given by Moses, but grace and truth came by Jesus Christ" (John 1:17). It is very important to see that the Law was temporary "until the seed should come"—and that Seed is Christ.

The Law was added "because of [for the sake of] transgressions. It was given to *reveal* not *remove* sin. It was not given to keep man from sin because sin had already come. It was to show man himself as being a natural, ugly, crude sinner before God. Any man who is honest will look at himself in the light of the Law and see himself guilty. It was not given to prove that all men were sinners, nor was it given (as many liberals are saying today) as a standard by which man becomes holy. Oh, my friend, you would never become holy this way, because, first of all, you can't keep the Law in your own strength.

Many folk think that man becomes a sinner when he commits a sinful act, that he is all right until he breaks down and commits sin. This is not true. It is because he is already a sinner that a man commits an act of sin. A man steals because he is a thief. A man lies because he is a liar. I find myself guilty of lying—although I blame it on other folk. I leave my house in the morning and the first person I meet says, "My, what a beautiful day!" And I say, "Yes, it is"—when truthfully it is a smoggy day here in pleasant California. I lie about it. Then he asks, "How are you feeling today?" Well, to be honest, I don't feel well, but I say, "Oh, I'm feeling fine." Right there in the first few minutes I have lied twice! It's just natural for us to be that way, my friend. Some of us commit more serious lying than that. Why do we do it? We have that fallen nature. And the Law was given to show that we are sinners, and that you and I need a mediator—One to stand between us and God, One to help us out.

> **Is the law then against the promises of God? God forbid: for if there had been a law given which could have given life, verily righteousness should have been by the law [Gal. 3:21].**

"Is the law then against the promises of God?" The expression "God forbid" means certainly not. Why? If there had been another way of saving sinners, God would have used that way. If He could have given a law by which sinners could be saved, He would have done so.

> **But the scripture hath concluded all under sin, that the promise by faith of Jesus Christ might be given to them that believe [Gal. 3:22].**

We have seen that the Law brought death—"The soul that sinneth, it shall die . . ." (Ezek. 18:20). The Scripture has "concluded all under sin"; therefore all died. What is needed, therefore, is life. We have seen that the Law brings death, which is all that it can do. It is not actually the degree of sin but the mere fact of sin that brings death. Hence, all are equally dead and equally in need. You may not have committed as great a sin as Stalin committed, but you and I have the same kind of nature that he had. In fact, it was Goethe, the great German writer, who made this statement: "I have never seen a crime committed but what I too might have committed that crime." He recognized he had that kind of a nature. It is not the degree of sin, but the very *fact* that we are sinners that brings death.

Let me illustrate this fact of sin and not the degree. Picture a building about twenty-four stories high. There are three men on top of the building, and the superintendent goes up to see them and warns, "Now be very careful, don't step off of this building or you will be killed. It will mean death for you." One of the fellows says, "This crazy superintendent is always trying to frighten people. I don't believe that if I step off this building I will die." So he deliberately walks to the edge of the building and steps off into the air. Suppose that when he passes the tenth floor, somebody looks out the window and asked him, "Well, how is it going?" And he says, "So far, so good." But, my friend, he hasn't arrived yet. There is death at the bottom. The superintendent was right. The man is killed. Now suppose another fellow becomes frightened at what the superintendent said. He runs for the elevator, or the steps, and accidentally slips. He skids right off the edge of the building and falls to the street below. He, too, is killed. The third fellow, we'll say, is thrown off the building by some gangsters because he is their enemy. He is killed. Now the man who was thrown off of the building is just as dead as the man who deliberately stepped off and the man who accidentally slipped off the building. All of these men broke the law of gravitation, and death was inevitable for all of them. It is the fact, you see, and not the degree. It is the fact that they went over the edge—they all broke the law of gravitation.

The question is, "Can the law of gravitation which took them down to death give them life?" It cannot. The Mosaic Law cannot give you life any more than a natural law can give you life after you have broken it and died. You cannot reverse the situation and come back from the street below to the top of the building and live, as it is done in running a movie in reverse. Death follows wherever sin comes. The law of sin knows nothing of extenuating circumstances. It knows nothing about mercy. It has no elasticity. It is inflexible, inexorable, and immutable. God's Word says, "The soul that sinneth, it shall die . . ." (Ezek. 18:20). To Adam and Eve in the Garden of Eden God said, "But of the tree of the knowledge of good and evil, thou shalt not eat of it: for in the day that thou eatest thereof thou shalt surely die" (Gen. 2:17). And in Exodus 34:7, He says that He ". . . will by no means clear the guilty. . . ." Therefore, all have sinned and by the Law we are all dead. The Law slew us. It is called by Paul a ". . . ministration of death . . ." (2 Cor. 3:7). It is a ministration of condemnation. The Law condemns all of us.

Can the Law bring life? My friend, the Law can no more bring life than a fall from a high roof can bring life to one who died by that fall. The purpose of the Law was never to give life. It was given to show us that we are guilty sinners before God.

"The scripture hath concluded all under sin, that the promise by faith of Jesus Christ might be given to them that believe" is a tremendous statement.

> **But before faith came, we were kept under the law, shut up unto the faith which should afterwards be revealed [Gal. 3:23].**

"Before faith came" means, of course, faith in Jesus Christ who died for us.

Until the Lord Jesus Christ came, the Law had in it mercy because it had a mercy seat. It had an altar where sacrifices for sin could be brought and forgiveness could be obtained. Mercy could be found there. All the sacrifices for sin pointed to Christ. Before faith came, Paul says, we were kept under the Law—"shut up unto the faith which should afterwards be revealed."

> **Wherefore the law was our schoolmaster to bring us unto Christ, that we might be justified by faith [Gal. 3:24].**

This is a remarkable section. Paul is making it very clear here that the Mosaic Law could not save. Romans 4:5 tells us, "But to him that worketh not, but believeth on him that justifieth the ungodly, his faith is counted for righteousness." God refused to accept the works of man for salvation. God says that all of our righteousnesses are as filthy rags

(Isa. 64:6). God refuses to accept law-keeping. The Law cannot save; it can only condemn. It was not given to save sinners but to let them know that they were sinners. The Law does not remove sin; it reveals sin. It will not keep you from sin, because sin has already come. The Law shows that man is not the way Hollywood portrays him—a sophisticated, refined, trained sinner. Man is actually an ugly sinner in the raw.

I want to use a homely illustration that I think might be helpful. I am going to take you to the bathroom. I hope you are not shocked—television does it every day, showing someone taking a bath or shower. I am confident that almost everyone has a bathroom, and in that bathroom is a washbasin with a mirror above it. That washbasin serves a purpose and so does the mirror. When you get dirt on your face, you go to the bathroom to remove it. Now you don't use the mirror to remove the dirt, do you? If you see a smudged spot on your face, and you lean over and rub your face against the mirror, and one of your loved ones sees you, he will call a psychiatrist and make an appointment to find out what is wrong with you. But, my friend, that won't happen because none of us is silly enough to try to remove dirt with a mirror.

Today, however, multitudes of people in our churches are rubbing up against the mirror of the law thinking they are going to remove their sin. The Word of God is a mirror which shows us who we are and what we are—that we are sinners and that we have come short of the glory of God. That is what the Law reveals. But, thank God, beneath the mirror there is a basin. As the hymn writer puts it,

> There is a fountain filled with blood
> Drawn from Immanuel's veins;
> And sinners plunged beneath that flood,
> Lose all their guilty stains.
> —William Cowper

That is where you remove the spot. It is the blood of the Lord Jesus Christ that cleanses. The Law proves man a sinner; it never makes him a saint. The Law was given, as Paul says in Romans, that every mouth might be stopped and the whole world become guilty before God (see Rom. 3:19).

"Wherefore the law was our schoolmaster," Paul says. Now he will go on to tell us what he means by this.

But after that faith is come, we are no longer under a schoolmaster [Gal. 3:25].

"Schoolmaster" is the Greek *paidagōgos*, and it doesn't mean school teacher. *Schoolmaster* is a good word, but it meant something quite different back in the days of Paul. It meant a servant or a slave who was part of a Roman household. Half of the Roman Empire was slave. Of the 120 million, 60 million were slaves. In the home of a patrician, a member of the Praetorian Guard, or the rich in the Roman Empire, were slaves that cared for the children. When a child was born into such a home, he was put in the custody of a servant or a slave who actually raised him. He put clean clothes on him, bathed him, blew his nose when it was necessary, and paddled him when he needed it. When the little one grew to a certain age and was to start to school, this servant was the one who got him up in the morning, dressed him, and took him to school. (That is where he got the name of *paidagōgos*. *Paid* has to do with the feet—and we get our word *pedal* from it; *agogos* means "to lead.") It means that he takes the little one by the hand, leads him to school, and turns him over to the school teacher. This servant, the slave, was not capable of teaching him beyond a certain age, so he took him to school.

Now what Paul is saying here is that the Law is our *paidagōgos*. The Law said, "Little fellow, I can't do any more for you. I now want to take you by the hand and bring you to the cross of Christ. You are lost. You need a Savior." The purpose of the Law is to bring men to Christ— not to give them an expanded chest so they can walk around claiming they keep the Law. You *know* you don't keep the Law; all you have to do is examine your own heart to know that.

For ye are all the children of God by faith in Christ Jesus [Gal. 3:26].

Paul is going to show in the remainder of this chapter, and in the first part of chapter 4, some of the benefits that come to us by trusting Christ that we could never receive under law. The Law never could give a believer the *nature* of a son of God. Christ can do that. Only faith in Christ can make us sons of God.

In this verse the word *children* is from the Greek *huios*, meaning "sons." Only faith in Christ can make us legitimate sons of God. I use the word *legitimate* for emphasis, because the only sons God has are legitimate sons. You are made a true son of God by faith in Christ, and that is *all* it takes. Not faith plus something equals salvation, but faith plus nothing makes you a son of God. Nothing else can make you a son of God. "For ye are all sons of God." How? "By faith in Christ Jesus."

An individual Israelite under the Law in the Old Testament was never a son, only a servant. God called the nation "Israel my son" (see Exod. 4:22), but the individual in that corporate nation was never called a son. He was called a servant of Jehovah. For example, Moses was on very intimate terms with God; yet God said of him, "Moses my servant is dead" (see Josh. 1:2). That was his epitaph. Also, although David was a man after God's own heart, God calls him "David my servant" (see 1 Kings 11:38).

My friend, even if you kept the Law, which you could not do, your righteousness would still be inferior to the righteousness of God. Sonship requires *His* righteousness, you see. The New Testament definitely tells us, "But as many as received him, to them gave he power to become the sons of God, even to them that believe on his name" (John 1:12). We are given the power (Greek *exousian*, meaning "the authority, the right") to become the sons of God by doing no more nor less than simply trusting Him. A Pharisee by the name of Nicodemus, religious to his fingertips (he had a God-given religion although it had gone to seed), followed the Law meticulously, yet he was not a son of God. Jesus said to him, "Ye must be born again" (John 3:7). I want to be dogmatic and very plain—neither your prayers, your fundamental separation, your gifts, nor your baptism will ever make you a son of God. Only faith in Christ can make you a son of God.

The most damnable heresy today is the "universal Fatherhood of

God and the universal brotherhood of man." It is this teaching of liberalism that has caused this nation to give away billions of dollars throughout the world, and because of it we are hated everywhere. All people are the children of God, they say, and so we have sat at council tables and have engaged in diplomatic squabbles with some of the biggest rascals the world has ever seen. We talk about being honest and honorable, that we are all the children of God, and we must act like sons of God. Well, the Lord Jesus Christ never said anything like that. He once looked at a group of religious rulers and said to them, "Ye are of your father the devil, and the lusts of your father ye will do . . ." (John 8:44). Now *I* did not say that; gentle Jesus said that. Evidently there were some people in His day who were not sons of God. My friend, I think the Devil still has a lot of children running around in this world today. They are not all the sons of God! The only way you can become a son of God is through faith in Jesus Christ.

For as many of you as have been baptized into Christ have put on Christ [Gal. 3:27].

I hope you realize that this verse is not a reference to water baptism. Water baptism is ritual baptism, and I feel that it is for every believer. Also I believe that the mode of water baptism should be by immersion (in spite of the fact that I am an ordained Presbyterian preacher), because immersion more clearly pictures real baptism, which is the baptism of the Holy Spirit. The baptism of the Holy Spirit places you in the body of believers. Paul says, "For by one Spirit are we all baptized into one body, whether we be Jews or Gentiles, whether we be bond or free; and have been all made to drink into one Spirit" (1 Cor. 12:13). This means that we are identified, we are put in reality and truth into the body of believers, the church. "For as many of you as have been baptized into Christ have put on Christ." God sees you in Christ. Therefore He sees you as perfect!

There is neither Jew nor Greek, there is neither bond nor free, there is neither male nor female: for ye are all one in Christ Jesus [Gal. 3:28].

In this body of believers "there is neither Jew nor Greek." In Christ are no racial lines. Any man in Christ is my brother, and I don't care about the color of his skin. It is the color of his heart that interests me. There are a lot of white people walking around with black hearts, my friend, and they are not my brothers. It is only in Christ Jesus that we are made one. Thank God, I receive letters from folk of every race. They call me brother and I call them brother—because we *are* brothers. We are one in Christ, and we will be together throughout eternity.

"There is neither bond nor free." In our day, capital and labor are at odds with one another. The only thing that could bring them together is Christ, of course.

"There is neither male nor female." Christ does what "women's lib" can never do. He can make us one in Christ. How wonderful it is!

And if ye be Christ's then are ye Abraham's seed, and heirs according to the promise [Gal. 3:29].

How can we be Abraham's descendants? Because of the fact that Abraham was saved by *faith,* and we are saved by *faith.* Abraham brought a little animal to sacrifice, which looked forward to the coming of the Son of God, the supreme sacrifice. In my day, Christ has already come, and I can look back in history and say, "Nineteen hundred years ago the Son of God came and died on the cross for me that I might have life, and I trust Him." Some time ago I had the privilege of speaking to a group of wonderful Jewish folk, and I started by saying, "Well, it is always a privilege for me to speak to the sons of Abraham." And they all smiled. Then I added, "Because I am a son of Abraham, too." They didn't all smile at that. In fact, some of them had a question mark on their faces, and rightly so. If I am in Christ and you are in Christ, then we belong to Abraham's seed, and we are heirs according to the promise. How wonderful this is!

CHAPTER 4

THEME: *Justification by faith; allegory of Hagar and Sarai*

Chapter 4 continues the section of justification by faith. Here we see that there is something else that comes through faith in Christ that we could never get by the works of the Law: it gives us the *position* of sons of God. It brings us to the place of full-grown sons. When we start out in the Christian life, we are babes and we are to grow to maturation. However, God gives us the position of a full-grown son to furnish us with a *capacity* that we would not otherwise have.

> **Now I say, That the heir, as long as he is a child, differeth nothing from a servant, though he be lord of all [Gal. 4:1].**

The word *child* in this verse is not the same as *child* in Galatians 3:26 where it is from the Greek word *huios*, meaning "son." Here it is *nepios*, meaning a little child without full power of speech. "The heir, as long as he is a child (a little one in the family), differeth nothing from a servant."

Again we will have to go back to the Roman customs to see Paul's illustration in action. In a Roman home servants had charge of different possessions of the master. Some had charge of the chattels, others of the livestock, others kept books for him, and others had charge of his children. When a little one was born into the home, the servants cared for him and dressed him in playclothes so that he didn't look any different from the children of the servants with whom he was playing. And he had to obey the servants just like the other children did.

> **But is under tutors and governors until the time appointed of the father [Gal. 4:2].**

"Until the time appointed of the father." What time was that? It was the time when the father recognized that his son was capable of making decisions of his own, and he brought him into the position of a full-grown son. Notice that it is the father who determined when his son reached the age of maturity. It wasn't an arbitrary law as we have in our society. It used to be that a young person became of age at twenty-one; now it's eighteen. I think that some folk are as mature at eighteen as they are at twenty-one. Also there are other folk who haven't reached maturity at sixty-five. But in Paul's day, it was the father who decided when the age of maturity was reached. Then they held a ceremony, known as the *toga virilis*, which gave him the position of a full-grown son in the family.

In a Roman home it must have worked something like this. Suppose the father is a centurion in Caesar's army. Caesar carries on a campaign way up in Gaul, and the man is up there several years—because that is where *our* ancestors were, and believe me, they were heathen! So he has trouble with them. He has to put them down, and it takes several years to do it. Because the army is pushing back the frontier of the Roman Empire, the father of the home is away for several years. Finally he returns home. He goes in to shave, and all of a sudden you hear him yell out, "Who's been using my razor?" Well, I tell you, all the servants come running, because he is the head of the house. They say to him, "Your son." He says, "You mean to tell me that my boy is old enough to use a razor!" The boy has grown to be a great big fellow. And the father says, "Bring him here." So they bring him in—he's a fine strapping boy—and the father says, "Well, now we must have the *toga virilis*, and we'll send out invitations to the grandmas, the grandpas, the aunts, and the uncles." So they all come in for the ceremony of the *toga virilis*, and that day the father puts around the boy a toga, a robe. That is what our Lord meant in His parable of the Prodigal Son. When the boy came home the father didn't receive him as just an ordinary son, he received him as a full-grown son, put the robe around him, and put a ring on his finger. The ring had on it the signet of his father, which was equivalent to his signature and gave him the father's authority. You could see that boy walking down the street now with that robe on. The servant better not say anything to correct him now, and he'd better not try to paddle him now. In fact, he'll be paddling the servant from here on because he has now reached the age of a full-grown son. That is what Paul meant when he went on to say:

Even so we, when we were children, were in bondage under the elements of the world [Gal. 4:3].

"Under the elements of the world" means under the Law. Paul is saying that it was the childhood of the nation Israel when they were under rules and regulations.

But when the fulness of the time was come, God sent forth his Son, made of a woman, made under the law [Gal. 4:4].

At the time determined by God, God the Father sent forth God the Son, born of a woman, born under the Law. Mary was a Jewish woman. Out here on the West Coast there is a woman who is saying that Jesus did not belong to any race. How absolutely puerile and senseless! It is an attempt to take a saccharine sweet position which has no meaning whatsoever. The woman at the well (as recorded in the fourth chapter of John's gospel) knew more than the woman out here today. She said, "How is it that thou, being a *Jew*, askest drink of me, which am a woman of Samaria? . . ." (John 4:9, italics mine). She thought He was a Jew, and our Lord didn't correct her; so I conclude that she was accurate. If you don't mind, I'll follow her rather than some of my contemporaries who try to play down the fact that Jesus, according to the flesh, was a Jew. He had a perfect humanity. He also was *God* manifest in the flesh. In my day that is being questioned. However, the only *historical* Jesus that we have is the One who is described in one of the oldest creeds of the church as "very man of very man and very God of very God." I agree with that creed because it is exactly what the Word of God teaches.

Now what was God's purpose in sending forth His Son?

To redeem them that were under the law, that we might receive the adoption of sons [Gal. 4:5].

God had a twofold purpose: (1) To redeem those under the Law. They were children under the Law. You see, the Law never made anyone a son of God. (2) That they might receive the adoption of sons.

Adoption has a meaning different from that of our contemporary society. We think of it in relationship with a couple that may not have children of their own. They go to a home where there are children for adoption and see a precious little baby there. Their hearts go out to him, and they adopt him in their family by going through legal action. When the little one becomes their child we call that adoption. However, the Roman custom in Paul's day was to adopt one's own son. That, you recall, was what was done in the *toga virilis* ceremony. *Adoption* (the Greek word is *huiothesia*) means "to place as a son." A believer is placed in the family of God as a full-grown son, capable of understanding divine truth.

In 1 Corinthians 2:9–10 we read, "But as it is written, Eye hath not seen, nor ear heard, neither have entered into the heart of man, the things which God hath prepared for them that love him. But God hath revealed them unto us by his Spirit: for the Spirit searcheth all things, yea, the deep things of God." This simply means that the truth in the Word of God can be interpreted only by the Spirit of God, and until He interprets it, man cannot understand it. The Holy Spirit alone can interpret the Word of God for us. That is what makes the difference today in certain men. A man can bring to the Word of God a brilliant mind. He can learn something about history, archaeology, and language. He can become an expert in Hebrew and Greek but can still miss the meaning. Why? Because the Spirit of God is the teacher. Even Isaiah the prophet said that: "For since the beginning of the world men have not heard, nor perceived by the ear, neither hath the eye seen, O God, beside thee, what he hath prepared for him that waiteth for him" (Isa. 64:4). If you want to know about Christ, only the Spirit of God can reveal Him to you. Even a mature Christian who has been in the Word for years is as helpless in studying the Bible as a newborn babe in Christ, because the Spirit of God will have to teach each of them.

I hope you will pardon my using a personal illustration. The only way I know a lot of these things is by pouring them through my own hopper—experiencing these truths myself. When I first started my schooling I was the youngest one in my class. When my father died, I had to quit school for three or four years in order to go to work. At that time I was the youngest one in my class. When I started my training for the ministry, I had those years of high school to make up, and when I went back to school, I was the oldest one in my class. When I entered seminary, I found that I was very ignorant of the Bible. I had never seen a Bible in my home. I had never heard a prayer in my home. I did not know the books of the Bible. I was ignorant, friend. No one could have been more ignorant of the Word of God than I was, and I felt it. I had to spend a lot of time memorizing the books of the Bible and many other basic things that I did not know when I first started studying. I developed an inferiority complex. When I preached as a young man, and I saw people with gray hair in the congregation, I would say to myself, *What I am going to say will be baby stuff for those folks because they really know the Bible.* However, I really had my eyes opened. I found out that there are still many people with gray hair who are babes in Christ. They have never grown up. The great truth which was given to me at this time was that the Spirit of God could teach me as a young believer as much as He could teach a mature Christian. We both could understand it if the Spirit of God was our teacher. This was a brand new truth for me, and it was a great encouragement as I was starting out in the ministry.

My friend, if you are a new believer, the same Spirit of God who is teaching me can teach you. If you are God's child, He has brought you into the position of a full-grown son, into the adoption. And, my friend, there is nothing quite as wonderful as that! That gave me confidence when I was a young believer and it gives me confidence to this good day. My friend, the Spirit of God will lead you and guide you into all truth if you *want* to know it, if you are willing for Him to be your teacher.

This brings us to the third thing that faith in Christ does for us that the Law could never do for us, which is the *experience* of sons of God.

And because ye are sons, God hath sent forth the Spirit of his Son into your hearts, crying, Abba, Father [Gal. 4:6].

"And because ye are sons" is a very strong statement.

Romans 8:16 says it this way, "The Spirit itself beareth witness with our spirit, that we are the children [the sons] of God." Paul continues to say in Romans, "But if the Spirit of him that raised up Jesus from the dead dwell in you, he that raised up Christ from the dead shall also quicken your mortal bodies by his Spirit that dwelleth in you. Therefore, brethren, we are debtors, not to the flesh, to live after the flesh. For if ye live after the flesh, ye shall die: but if ye through the Spirit do mortify the deeds of the body, ye shall live [as sons]. For as many as are led by the Spirit of God, they are the sons of God" (Rom. 8:11–14). If you are a child of God, you will want to be led by the Spirit of God. The flesh may get a victory in your life, but it will never make you happy. You will never be satisfied with it, because ". . . ye have not received the spirit of bondage again to fear." You don't need to say, "My, I'm not living as I should live, and I wonder if I'm a child of God." My friend, "ye have received the Spirit of adoption, whereby we cry, Abba, Father. The Spirit itself beareth witness with our spirit, that we are the children of God" (Rom. 8:15–16). This passage in the Epistle to the Romans is the unabridged edition of the parallel passage in Galatians. I wanted you to see all of it.

The word *Abba* was not translated, I am told, because the translators of the King James Version had a great reverence for the Word of God. When they came to the word *Abba*, they didn't dare translate it into English because it was such an intimate word. It could be translated "my daddy." God is my wonderful heavenly Father, but I would hesitate to call him "daddy."

Wherefore thou art no more a servant, but a son; and if a son, then an heir of God through Christ [Gal. 4:7].

The Spirit, therefore, gives us an experience of being a son of God, whereby we can cry out—not just saying the word or putting on a false "piosity"—and call God our *Father*, because the Spirit is bearing witness with our spirit. This gives us the experience of being a son of God.

There are many folk who believe that the only way you can have an experience is either by reaching a high degree of sanctification—you've got to become holy—or you have to seek the baptism of the Holy Spirit, as they call it. They insist that if you don't get up to that level, you will never have an experience. My friend, let me assure you, if you are a new believer or a weak believer, that you can have an experience as a son of God without reaching those levels, because sonship comes to you through faith in Jesus Christ. When folk have reached a high level of spirituality, they tend to think they are superior to the rest of us. However, we are always God's foolish little children. We are always filled with ignorance and stubbornness and sin and fears and weaknesses. *We* are never wonderful; *He* is wonderful. The Lord Jesus is wonderful, and faith in Him will give us an experience. I believe in experience, and I feel that a great many folk today need an experience with God.

Paul Rader, who was one of the greatest preachers this country has ever produced, used some very striking expressions. One day on the platform he said, "The old nature that you and I have is just like an old dead cat. What you need to do is reach down and get that old dead cat by the tail and throw it as far away as you can." I can say "amen" to that. I wish I could get rid of my old nature. One day Dr. Chafer heard him use this illustration, and he said to him afterward, "Paul, you forget that the old dead cat has nine lives. When you throw him away, he is going to be right back tomorrow." We will never become perfect saints of God, but we can experience being sons of God by faith in Jesus Christ. "And because ye are sons, God hath sent forth the Spirit of his Son into your hearts, crying, Abba, Father. Wherefore thou art no more a servant, but a son; and if a son, then an heir of God through Christ." Many times you and I plod along in our Christian lives, and we don't have an experience with God. Sometimes life becomes very drab and a little monotonous. But there are other times, especially when God puts us on trial and really tests us, that we have a wonderful experience with our Heavenly Father.

I recall when I was taken to the hospital to be operated on for cancer. No one was ever as frightened as I was because I am a coward, and I don't like hospitals. (I thank God for them, but I still don't like them.) I put on that funny looking nightgown they give you that is open in the back instead of the front, and I was trying to get up into the bed. I just couldn't make it. A nurse came in and said, "What's the matter? Are you sick?" I said, "No, I'm scared to death!" Then, when she came to get me ready for the operation, I said, "Just let me have a few moments alone." I had visited in that hospital many times as a pastor—in fact, several hundred times. Now I turned my face to the wall just like Hezekiah did and I said, "Lord, I want you to know that I have been here many times, and I have patted people on the hand and told them that You would be with them. As their pastor I prayed for them and then walked out. But I am not walking out today. I am going to have to stay and be operated on myself. I don't know what the outcome will be." I had some things I wanted to tell God. I wanted to tell Him how He ought to work it out. But I just welled up inside, and said, "My Father, I'm in Your hands. Whatever You want done, You do it. You're my Father." He was so wonderful to me. That is when He becomes a reality, my beloved. We need to experience Him as our Abba, Father. "The Spirit itself beareth witness with our spirit, that we are the children [sons] of God" (Rom. 8:16). Now, I don't wish you any trouble, but I think it is generally in times of trouble that God makes Himself real to us. I hope that someday you will have such an experience with our wonderful heavenly Father.

There is one illustration I want to use before I move on. John G. Paton was a pioneer missionary in the New Hebrides. He went to the mission field as a young man with a young bride. When their first child was born, the child died and the wife died. He buried them with his own hands. Because he was among cannibals, he sat over the grave for many days and nights to prevent them from digging up the bodies and eating them. His testimony was that if the Lord Jesus Christ had not made Himself real to him during that time, he would have gone mad.

God makes Himself real during times of distress. When Paul was in prison, he could say, "At my first answer no man stood with me, but all men forsook me: I pray God that it may not be laid to their charge. Notwithstanding the Lord stood with me, and strengthened me . . ." (2 Tim. 4:16–17). The Lord stood by Paul. He stood by John Paton. He stood by me. He will stand by you. How reassuring it is to have a Father like that! At such a time He says, ". . . I will never leave thee, nor forsake thee" (Heb. 13:5). I trust you are His son.

Howbeit then, when ye knew not God, ye did service unto them which by nature are no gods [Gal. 4:8].

Paul is speaking of the fact that the Galatians had been idolaters. When I visited that Galatian country in Asia Minor, where the seven churches were located, I saw how completely the population then was given over to the worship of idols. Paul describes idols as vanities— "nothings." In 1 Corinthians 12:2 Paul called them "dumb idols." They were nothing and could say nothing. He is telling the Galatians that idols are not real and cannot make themselves real to those who worship them.

But now, after that ye have known God, or rather are known of God, how turn ye again to the weak and beggarly elements, whereunto ye desire again to be in bondage? [Gal. 4:9].

"Known of God" actually means *approved* of God or to be *acknowledged* of God. They had come to Christ through faith and God accepts that. Most of the believers in the Galatian churches were Gentiles. Now that they were Christians, they were turning to the Mosaic Law, which is, as Paul says, like going back into the idolatry they came out of.

Ye observe days, and months, and times, and years [Gal. 4:10].

"Ye observe days," meaning the sabbath days. Paul said to the Colossians, "Let no man therefore judge you in meat, or in drink, or in respect of an holyday, or of the new moon, or of the sabbath days" (Col. 2:16).

"Months" probably refers to the observance of the "new moon" practiced by the people of Israel in the time of the kings. The prophets warned them against it.

"Times" should be translated *seasons,* meaning feasts. God had given Israel seven feasts, but they all had pointed to the Lord Jesus Christ.

"Years" of course would refer to the sabbatic years. The observance of all these things would put these gentile believers completely back under the Mosaic Law.

Today I hear legalists claim they are keeping the Mosaic Law, yet they are keeping only the sabbath day. My friend, all the law comes in one package, including the sabbatic year and the Year of Jubilee. James in his epistle said, "For whosoever shall keep the whole law, and yet offend in one point, he is guilty of all" (James 2:10). That is, he is guilty of being a lawbreaker.

I am afraid of you, lest I have bestowed upon you labour in vain [Gal. 4:11].

Paul is saying, in a nice way, that he thinks he has wasted his time among them. Since they have been saved by grace, their returning to the Law is the same as returning to their former idolatry. He reminded them that they had not known God by means of the Mosaic Law but by faith in Jesus Christ.

We have come now to a personal section (vv. 12–18). It is a polite word that Paul is injecting in this epistle.

Brethren, I beseech you, be as I am; for I am as ye are: ye have not injured me at all [Gal. 4:12].

"Be as I am" is better translated *become* as I am. The Galatians had been listening to false teachers, and they were looking upon Paul as an enemy because he told them the truth. Paul is saying, "We are all on the same plane. We are all believers, all in the body of Christ. In view of this we ought to be very polite to one another."

Ye know how through infirmity of the flesh I preached the gospel unto you at the first [Gal. 4:13].

Now Paul makes an appeal to them on the basis of his thorn in the flesh. What was that thorn? Let's read on.

And my temptation which was in my flesh ye despised not, nor rejected; but received me as an angel of God, even as Christ Jesus [Gal. 4:14].

"And my temptation which was in my flesh" means the *trial,* which elsewhere he calls his thorn in the flesh.

Where is then the blessedness ye spake of? for I bear you record, that, if it had been possible, ye would have plucked out your own eyes, and have given them to me [Gal. 4:15].

Probably Paul's thorn in the flesh was some sort of eye trouble, and it evidently made him very unattractive. I cannot conceive of them wanting to pluck out their eyes and give them to Paul if what he really needed was another leg. Apparently Paul had an eye disease which is common in that land and is characterized by excessive pus that runs out of the eyes. You can well understand how unattractive that would be to look at while he was ministering to them. Paul says, "You just ignored it, and received me so wonderfully when I preached the gospel to you."

Am I therefore become your enemy, because I tell you the truth? [Gal. 4:16].

I had always wanted to place on the pulpit, facing the preacher, the words, "Sir, we would see Jesus." A very fine officer of the church I served in downtown Los Angeles did this for me after he heard me express this desire. There is another verse I wanted to place on the audience side of the pulpit, but I never had the nerve to do it. It is these words of Paul: "Am I therefore become your enemy, because I tell you the truth?" As you know, many folk today really don't want the preacher to tell the truth from the pulpit. They would much rather he would say something complimentary that would smooth their feathers and make them feel good. We all like to have our backs rubbed, and there is a lot of back-rubbing from the contemporary pulpit rather than the declaration of the truth.

> **They zealously affect you, but not well; yea, they would exclude you, that ye might affect them.**
>
> **But it is good to be zealously affected always in a good thing, and not only when I am present with you [Gal. 4:17–18].**

These verses are more easily understood in the American Standard Version which says, "They zealously seek you in no good way; nay, they desire to shut you out, that ye may seek them. But it is good to be zealously sought in a good matter at all times, and not only when I am present with you." Paul is saying that it is good to seek that which is the very best, but these Judaizers are after you in order to scalp you. They want to put your scalp on their belt and be able to say, "We were over at Galatia, and we had so many converts"—which, of course, would not be actually true. Paul had somewhat the same thing to say to the Corinthian believers: "Truly the signs of an apostle were wrought among you in all patience, in signs, and wonders, and mighty deeds. For what is it wherein ye were inferior to other churches, except it be that I myself was not burdensome to you? forgive me this wrong. Behold, the third time I am ready to come to you; and I will not be burdensome to you: for I seek not yours, but you: for the children ought not to lay up for the parents, but the parents for the children. And I will very gladly spend and be spent for you; though the more abundantly I love you, the less I be loved" (2 Cor. 12:12–15).

You see, this same crowd of Judaizers had gone to Corinth. The Corinthian believers had loved Paul also, and Paul had to warn them of these men. False teachers are often very attractive. I am amazed at the very fine presentation the cults make. I have watched them on television programs that are done to perfection. That is the subtle part of it. Everything is beautiful to look at, and those taking part are attractive individuals. Also they present a certain amount of truth. For example, I listened to a man who is a liberal give the Christmas story during the Christmas season. No one could have told it better than he did. It was an excellent presentation. But when he began to interpret it, I realized that he didn't even believe in the virgin birth of Christ. You see, the warning of Paul both to the Galatian and Corinthian believers is very timely for our generation also.

ALLEGORY OF HAGAR AND SARAI

This chapter concludes with an allegory of Hagar and Sarai. All is contrast in this section between these two women. Hagar, and every reference to her under other figures of speech, represents the Law. Sarai, and every reference to her under other figures of speech, represents faith in Christ.

My little children, of whom I travail in birth again until Christ be formed in you [Gal. 4:19].

Paul addresses his allegory to the Galatian believers by using this tender expression, "My little children," *children* is the Greek word *teknia* meaning "born ones." Paul has a very tender heart, and he likens himself to a mother.

I desire to be present with you now, and to change my voice; for I stand in doubt of you [Gal. 4:20].

Paul wanted to be present so that he could speak differently. He was deeply concerned about these people. He had been using strong language in his letter, but you can see his tender heart.

Tell me, ye that desire to be under the law, do ye not hear the law? [Gal. 4:21].

There are people who talk about the Ten Commandments or some legal system, but they don't talk about the *penalty* imposed by the Law. They don't present the Law in the full orb of its ministry of condemnation. Notice what happened when God called Moses to the mountain to give the Law: "And it came to pass on the third day in the morning, that there were thunders and lightnings, and a thick cloud upon the mount, and the voice of the trumpet exceeding loud; so that all the people that was in the camp trembled. And Moses brought forth the people out of the camp to meet with God; and they stood at the nether part of the mount. And mount Sinai was altogether on a smoke, because the LORD descended upon it in fire: and the smoke thereof ascended as the smoke of a furnace, and the whole mount quaked greatly. And when the voice of the trumpet sounded long, and waxed louder and louder, Moses spake, and God answered him by a voice. And the LORD came down upon mount Sinai, on the top of the mount: and the LORD called Moses up to the top of the mount; and Moses went up. And the LORD said unto Moses, Go down, charge the people, lest they break through unto the LORD to gaze, and many of them perish" (Exod. 19:16–21).

God told the people to stand back, actually to stand afar off, when He gave Moses the Law. Exodus 20:18–19 says, "And all the people saw the thunderings, and the lightnings, and the noise of the trumpet, and the mountain smoking: and when the people saw it, they removed, and stood afar off. And they said unto Moses, Speak thou with us, and we will hear: but let not God speak with us, lest we die."

We cannot conceive of how holy God is. You and I are renegades in God's universe. We are in the position of being lost sinners in God's universe with no capacity to follow or obey Him. Romans 8:6 says, "For to be carnally minded is death; but to be spiritually minded is life and peace." The carnal mind is enmity against God. My friend, the world is against God; it is not for God. The world is not getting better. It is becoming more evil each day, and it has been bad since the day God put Adam and Eve out of the Garden of Eden. Romans 8;7 goes on to say, "Because the carnal mind is enmity against God: for it is not subject to the law of God, neither indeed can be." No wonder the children of Israel trembled and moved away from the mountain and said, "We will *die*."

Now, my friend, God is high and holy and lifted up, and He dwells in glory. You and I are down here making mud pies in the world because physically we are made out of mud. We creatures walk about here on earth and have the audacity to walk contrary to the will of God! The carnal mind is enmity against God. That is man's position in the world.

Paul says, "Listen to the Law. You haven't even heard it yet." It was true. The Galatians had not actually heard the Law. The giving of the Law was not beautiful and cozy, but terrifying. The Galatians seemed to want to be under law so Paul was going to let them hear it.

For it is written, that Abraham had two sons, the one by a bondmaid, the other by a freewoman [Gal. 4:22].

Using an illustration from the life of Abraham (Gen. 16; 17; 18; 20; 21), Paul is going to make a contrast between these two boys that were born, one to Hagar and one to Sarai. One was the son of a bondwoman; the other was the son of a freewoman. The freewoman represents grace, and the bondwoman represents the Mosaic Law. He is going to point out the contrast between them in what he calls an allegory.

Paul is not saying that the story of Abraham is an allegory—some have interpreted this statement as meaning that—but Paul is saying that the incident of the two women who bore Abraham sons *contains* an allegory. It has a message for us today.

But he who was of the bondwoman was born after the flesh; but he of the freewoman was by promise [Gal. 4:23].

"He who was of the bondwoman was born after the flesh." The Code of Hammurabi, which governed the culture in Abraham's day, stated that the son of a slave woman was a slave. So even though Ishmael was Abraham's son, he was a slave.

"He of the freewoman was by promise." Isaac was a miracle child, that is, his birth was miraculous. Abraham was too old to father a child, and Paul says that the womb of Sarai was dead. She had passed the age of childbearing. The womb of Sarai was like a tomb, and out of death God brought life.

> **Which things are an allegory: for these are the two covenants; the one from the mount Sinai, which gendereth to bondage, which is Agar [Gal. 4:24].**

"Which things are an allegory," meaning that these events in Abraham's life *contain* an allegory. Paul is going to draw a lesson from it.

"For these are the two covenants"—the first is the covenant of the Law which Moses received from God on Mount Sinai.

"Which is Agar" (*Agar* is the Greek form of the name *Hagar*). Paul compares Hagar to Mount Sinai which is synonymous with the Mosaic Law.

> **For this Agar is mount Sinai in Arabia, and answereth to Jerusalem which now is, and is in bondage with her children [Gal. 4:25].**

In Paul's allegory Hagar is Mount Sinai which corresponds to Jerusalem (the earthly Jerusalem of Paul's day), because she was still in slavery with her children. In other words, Jerusalem (representing the nation of Israel) was still under the bondage of the Law.

> **But Jerusalem which is above is free, which is the mother of us all [Gal. 4:26].**

"Jerusalem which is above" is the New Jerusalem which is presented to us in the twentieth chapter of Revelation as it comes down from God out of heaven. As old Jerusalem is the mother city of those under the law, so the New Jerusalem is the mother city of the believer under grace. The believer neither here nor hereafter has any connection with legalism.

For it is written, Rejoice, thou barren that bearest not; break forth and cry, thou that travailest not: for the desolate hath many more children than she which hath an husband [Gal. 4:27].

From Sarai (who was barren until the birth of Isaac) there came more descendants than ever came from Hagar. Today the Arabs are fewer than the children of Israel. In this allegory, Paul is saying that God is saving under grace more members of the human family than He ever saved under the Mosaic Law by the sacrificial system.

Now we, brethren, as Isaac was, are the children of promise [Gal. 4:28].

Believers today are also children of promise. Our birth is a *new* birth, which comes about by our believing God's promise: "For God so loved the world, that he gave his only begotten Son, that whosoever believeth in him should not perish, but have everlasting life" (John 3:16). God has said that if we trust Him, we'll be born again. "Being born again, not of corruptible seed, but of incorruptible, by the word of God, which liveth and abideth for ever" (1 Pet. 1:23).

But as then he that was born after the flesh persecuted him that was born after the Spirit, even so it is now [Gal. 4:29].

My friend, the legalist hates the gospel of the free grace of God. When I was first ordained to the ministry, I preached a sermon on prophecy and made the comment that preaching on prophecy would get me into trouble. After the service, an elder came to me and said, "Vernon, you are mistaken. Preaching on prophecy will never get you into trouble. In fact, you'll generally get a good crowd. People like to hear prophecy. But if you preach the grace of God, you're going to get into trouble." This is the reason that the gospel is trimmed down as it is today. I hear very little gospel, that is, the pure grace of God, preached these days. And I know why—if you preach that, you get a barrage of criticism. Folk insist that I have to also *do* something or *seek* something from another source—from the Holy Spirit, for instance, or go through some ceremony in order to receive something that I did not get when I trusted Jesus Christ. My friend, to say that is calling Christ a curse. If you have to add anything to what He did for you, then His death on the cross was in vain. Christ was made a curse for us; but if you don't accept what He did for you, you are saying that you are not guilty, but that He is guilty. These words of Paul are as relevant in our day as they were in his day: "But as then he that was born after the flesh persecuted him that was born after the Spirit, even so it is now." The natural man hates the gospel of the grace of God. My friend, it is *in* us to hate it, because it doesn't require any *doing* on our part. Rather, it glorifies Christ and turns our eyes to Him.

> **Nevertheless what saith the scripture? Cast out the bondwoman and her son: for the son of the bondwoman shall not be heir with the son of the freewoman [Gal. 4:30].**

God commanded the expulsion of the bondwoman and her son (see Gen. 21:10). Today God is saying to you and to me, "Get rid of your legalism. Put all of the emphasis on Jesus Christ."

> **So then, brethren, we are not children of the bond-woman, but of the free [Gal. 4:31].**

Abraham could not have both the son of Hagar and the son of Sarai. He had to make a choice. Paul is saying that you can't be saved by law and grace. You have to make a choice. If you try to be saved by Christ and also by law, you are not saved.

Let me ask you, have you really trusted Christ, or are you carrying a spare tire on your little omnibus; that is, do you feel that you are *doing* something or *being* something or trying to *attain* to something which adds to what Jesus Christ did for you on the cross? If you do, forget it and look to Christ alone; receive everything from Him. He is our Savior. He is our Lord. He is to receive all praise and glory.

CHAPTER 5

THEME: *Sanctification by the Spirit; saved by faith and living by law perpetrates falling from grace; saved by faith and walking in the Spirit produces fruit of the Spirit*

SANCTIFICATION BY THE SPIRIT

This brings us to the third major division in Galatians after the Introduction. The first section was *personal*, and it was important for us to know the personal experience Paul had had. Following this was the *doctrinal* section of justification by faith in which Paul insisted that our salvation must rest upon *God's* salvation and that there is only one gospel.

We come now to the practical side, which is sanctification by the Spirit. Justification is by faith; sanctification is by the Spirit of God. Scripture tells us, however, that the Lord Jesus Christ has been made unto us sanctification—that is, God sees us complete in Him. Regardless of how good you become, you will never meet His standard. You will never be like Christ in this life. Christ is the only One about whom God said, ". . . This is my beloved Son, in whom I am well pleased" (Matt. 3:17). But the body of believers, the church, has been put *in* Christ. He is the Head of the body; those of us who are believers are His body in the world today—and we should represent Him, by the way.

The method of sanctification is by the Spirit. In this section we see the Spirit versus the flesh. Either it is a do-it-yourself Christian life or somebody else will have to do it *through* you. His method is doing it through you.

In this section we see liberty versus bondage. Any legal system puts you under bondage, and you have to follow it meticulously.

Let me illustrate this from my own experience with civil law with which all of us are familiar.

As I was driving my car early one Sunday morning, I came to a corner where there was a stop sign. It was so early, no one else was out; I looked up and down the street, but I didn't stop—I just crawled through. A traffic officer appeared behind me; he came up to me and asked, "Did you see that stop sign?" I said, "Yes, I saw the sign; I just didn't see *you!*" Then he asked, "Do you know what that sign means?" And he proceeded to give me a primary lesson in law. He said, "Stop means *stop.*" Well, I already knew that; I just wasn't doing it. Believe me, the law puts you in bondage. And if you are going to drive a car, you had better be under law, because a lot of folk drive through stop signs and cause accidents. Stop means stop. I agreed with him on everything except one: I didn't think I deserved a ticket. I argued with him about that. And he was a very nice fellow; he saw my point. He said, "Well, I grant you that there is nobody out this morning, but hereafter you stop. Will you?" I assured him that I would stop. Ever since then, even if it is early Sunday morning, I stop at that sign—and wherever I see a stop sign. Now that is legalism. It is an example of legalism that we all understand.

SAVED BY FAITH AND LIVING BY LAW
PERPETRATES FALLING FROM GRACE

Paul begins on the note of liberty which we have in Christ. His subject in these first fifteen verses is "Saved by faith and living by law perpetrates falling from grace." This is what it means to fall from grace: you are saved by faith, then you drop down to a *law* level to live. We will see this illustrated as we move into this section.

Stand fast therefore in the liberty wherewith Christ hath made us free, and be not entangled again with the yoke of bondage [Gal. 5:1].

He is saying here that not only are we saved by faith rather than by law, but law is not to be the rule of life for the believer. We are not to live by law at all. The law principle is not the rule for Christian living. Paul is saying that since we have been saved by grace we are to continue on in this way of living. Grace supplies the indwelling and filling of the

Spirit to enable us to live on a higher plane than law demanded. This all is our portion when we trust Christ as Savior. It is in Christ that we receive everything—salvation and sanctification. Don't tell me I need to seek a second blessing. When I came to Christ, I got everything I needed. Paul tells me that I have been blessed with all spiritual blessings in Christ Jesus. Let's believe Him and start trusting. Let's stop trying some legal system or rote of rules.

We have a liberty in Christ. He does not put us under some little legal system. We do not use the Ten Commandments as a law of life. I don't mean we are to break the Ten Commandments—I think we all understand that breaking most of them (i.e., thou shalt not kill; thou shalt not steal, etc.) would lead to our arrest by local authorities. Certainly Christians do not break the Commandments, but we are called to a higher level to live. That level is where there is liberty in Christ. I have a liberty in Jesus Christ, and that liberty is not a rule, but a principle. It is that I am to please Him. My conduct should be to please Jesus Christ—not to please you, not to please any organization, but only to please Him. That is the liberty that we have in the Lord Jesus Christ. "Stand fast therefore in the liberty wherewith Christ hath made us free, and be not entangled again with the yoke of bondage."

Behold, I Paul say unto you, that if ye be circumcised, Christ shall profit you nothing [Gal. 5:2].

Circumcision was the badge of the Law. A badge indicates to what organization or lodge you belong. Perhaps Christians should wear a badge because that is about the only way you could tell that some people are Christians. But Paul says that if you so much as put on the badge of the Law, which is circumcision, then Christ does not profit you anything.

Let me use a homely illustration to prove the point. Years ago a tonic called Hadacol was advertised. I don't think it is sold any more. I am not sure of the details, but they found it was about seventy-five percent alcohol. A lot of people were using it. The company that made it was giving out glowing testimonials about its product. Now suppose a testimonial read something like this: "I took 513 bottles of your medicine. Before I began using Hadacol, I could not walk. Now I am able to run, and I am actually able to fly! I really have improved. But I think you ought to know that during that time I also concocted a bottle of my own medicine and used it also." Now, my friend, that final sentence certainly muddied the water. There is no way to tell if it was the 513 bottles of Hadacol that cured him or his own concoction. The minute you put something else into the formula, you are not sure.

Now notice carefully what Paul is saying. If you trust Christ plus something else you are not saved. If you go so far as to be circumcised, which is only the badge of the Law, or if you go through some other experience and rest your salvation on that, "Christ shall profit you nothing." How can He profit you anything when you have made up a bottle of your own concoction rather than trusting Him alone for your salvation?

The way Dr. Lewis Sperry Chafer put it always impressed me. It was something like this: "I want to so trust Christ that when I come into His presence and He asks me, 'Why are you here?' I can say, 'I am here because I trusted You as my Savior.' If He asked me, 'Well, that is commendable, but what have you done? I happen to know that you were president of a seminary, and that you were baptized. You were also a member of a church. You did many fine things during your ministry,' then I would reply, 'It is all true, but I never trusted in any of it for salvation. I trusted only You, my Lord.'" My friend, is that the way you are trusting Christ? Paul makes it very strong when he says, "if ye be circumcised, Christ shall profit you nothing." If you trust anything other than Christ, you are not a Christian.

For I testify again to every man that is circumcised, that he is a debtor to do the whole law [Gal. 5:3].

You cannot draw out of the Law just those things that you like. You cannot leave out the penalties and a great deal of the detail. You must take the whole Law or nothing. I am delighted that I am not under the Law. I have liberty in Christ! I must confess that I have a problem of always pleasing Him, but He is the One I am trying to please. I am not following some legal system. "For I testify again to every man that is circumcised, that he is a debtor to do the whole law."

Christ is become of no effect unto you, whosoever of you are justified by the law; ye are fallen from grace [Gal. 5:4].

If you have been saved by trusting Christ, then go down to the low level of living by the Law, you have fallen from grace. This is what "falling from grace" actually means. I can remember as a student in a denominational seminary hearing one theologian say, "Falling from grace is the doctrine which the Methodists believe and the Presbyterians practice." However, falling from grace does not mean falling into some open sin or careless conduct, and by so doing forfeiting your salvation so that you have to be saved all over again. It has no reference to that at all. "Falling from grace" is the opposite of "once saved always saved," although both expressions are unfortunate terminology. Paul deals with this matter of falling from grace in the remainder of this chapter. He also deals with it in his Epistle to the Romans. In Romans he begins with man in the place of total bankruptcy—without righteousness, completely depraved, as unprofitable as rotten fruit. Man is a sinner before God. Then at the conclusion of Romans you see man in the service of God and being admonished to perform certain things. Not only is he admonished to perform certain things, he is completely separated to God, and he must be obedient to God.

There are two mighty works of God which stand between the man in his fallen condition and man in service to God. These are salvation and sanctification. As we have seen, salvation is justification by faith. That is all-important. Sanctification means that after you are saved you are to come up to a new plane of living. I think the greatest fallacy is to believe that service is essential in the Christian life, that you must get busy immediately. The early church was more concerned with its manner of life, and that life was a witness to the world. Today the outside world is looking at the church and passing it by because we are busy, as busy as termites, but we do not have lives to back up our witness. Rather than concentrating on trying to do good, we ought to live "good." If we are pleasing Christ, we will be doing good also. I think there is more about sanctification in the Epistles to the Romans and to the Galatians than anything else.

Now how does God make a saved sinner good? Well, He gives him a new nature. Then he is to keep the Law? Oh, no. Emphatically no. This doesn't mean he is to break the Law, but he is called to live on a higher plane. There is no good in the old nature. Paul found that out, and he also found out from experience that there is no power in the new nature. As to salvation he said, "For I know that in me (that is, in my flesh,) dwelleth no good thing," and he also found out, ". . . to *will* is present with me; but how to perform that which is good I find not" (Rom. 7:18, italics mine). And he cries out as a saved man, "O wretched man that I am! who shall deliver me from the body of this death?" (Rom. 7:24). He is not afraid that he is going to lose his salvation, but he is a defeated Christian. God gives a new principle. We will find in this chapter that the new principle is the fruit of the Spirit.

Living the Christian life by this method for some Christians is as farfetched as living on the moon! They never expect to live there. Perhaps they have never even heard about the possibility. My friend, this is the life He wants us to live—by *faith*. We are saved by grace; we are to live by grace.

For we through the Spirit wait for the hope of righteousness by faith [Gal. 5:5].

"The hope of righteousness" is the only prophetic reference in the entire epistle. This is quite remarkable, because in all Paul's epistles he has something to say about the rapture of the church or about Christ's coming to earth to establish His kingdom. But here in Galatians he says only this: "the hope of righteousness by faith," and the hope of righteousness is the Lord Jesus Christ. The only hope is the blessed hope, and Christ is made unto us righteousness.

As I have pointed out, the Epistle to the Galatians was very important to Martin Luther and to the other reformers. This is one of the reasons, I am confident, that they spent so little time on prophecy.

All the schools of prophecy—the premillennialists, the amillennialists, and the postmillennialists have quoted Martin Luther and the other reformers on this matter of prophecy. But I do not think that there was any development of prophecy beyond what the early church wrote until the twentieth century. In this twentieth century there has been tremendous development in prophecy. The Bible institutes were probably the beginning of this movement, then two or three of our seminaries that have emphasized the premillennial position have forced the others to study prophecy. Actually, amillennialists are just a group of the postmillennialists who were forced into the study of prophecy and came up with the theory of amillennialism. Of course, they have been great at quoting the fathers of the postapostolic period. They say, Augustine said thus and so, and he did say it. He was attempting to build the kingdom here, that is, the church was going to bring in the kingdom. This led to postmillennialism, which was, of course, a false position. I don't feel that we should criticize Augustine for that since he was living in a day when the study of prophecy was not developed. The person of Christ was the great subject during his time, as salvation was the great subject later on.

Therefore the fact that Paul has only this brief reference to prophecy in his Epistle to the Galatians is understandable, since his emphasis is on the gospel and the Christian life. It is important to note the priorities in any book of the Bible and also the priorities that were in existence in any given period. Failing to do this leads to misinterpretation and misunderstanding which is the case in quoting church fathers on the matter of prophecy. After all, the authorities on prophecy are Paul, Peter, James, Matthew, Mark, and Luke. We need to note what they have written on the subject of prophecy. But to the Galatians Paul writes simply, "For we through the Spirit wait for the hope of righteousness by faith." I think Paul's reason for saying this here is that believers are not going to reach perfection in this life. And the greatest imperfection I know of today is to *think* you have reached perfection. Folk who think they are perfect are imperfect like the rest of us—but they don't know it.

For in Jesus Christ neither circumcision availeth any thing, nor uncircumcision; but faith which worketh by love [Gal. 5:6].

No legal apparatus will produce a Christian life. The formula is simple: "faith which worketh by love." As we advance in Galatians, Paul will give us the modus operandi, but let us remember that it is a simple formula: "Faith which worketh by love." That is the way to live the Christian life. Faith will work by love. Love will be the fruit of the Holy Spirit.

> **Ye did run well; who did hinder you that ye should not obey the truth? [Gal. 5:7].**

Paul chides the Galatians. He is giving them a gentle rebuke. They were doing excellently until the Judaizers came along. "The truth" is the gospel, of course, and the Lord Jesus Christ in person.

> **This persuasion cometh not of him that calleth you [Gal. 5:8].**

It didn't come from Christ but from a different source.

> **A little leaven leaveneth the whole lump [Gal. 5:9].**

In Scripture, both Old and New Testaments, leaven is always used as a principle of evil. In Matthew 13:33, when the woman hid leaven in three measures of meal, the leaven was not the gospel. It may be the kind of a "gospel" that is passing around today as legal tender, but it is still evil. In fact, Paul says that it is no gospel at all. The Lord Jesus warned His disciples of the leaven of the Pharisees (see Matt. 16:6). I think we need to be warned today of the leaven of legalism. It is an awful thing. Legalism says that when Christ died on the cross for you and me, over nineteen hundred years ago, He did not give us a full package of salvation, but that I have to go through a ritual of baptism or seek something else from the Holy Spirit to get the rest of it. My friend, I received it *all* when I accepted Christ. Now I may have experiences after I am saved, but that does not add to my salvation. Christ is the One who wrought out our salvation. The Lord Jesus said that the woman would take the leaven and hide it in three measures of meal, symbolic of the gospel. In other words, leaven has been hidden in the gospel—and that makes it palatable to the natural man.

I was brought up in the South, and I never knew there was any kind of biscuits but *hot* biscuits. My mother used to bake them every day. Even yet I can see those biscuits in the dough stage, rising on the back of the stove. When they reached a certain height, she stuck them in the oven. They had leaven in them. When the biscuits were done, I would put butter and honey on them. There was nothing better! That is still my favorite dessert. There is a lot of leaven being put in the gospel today to make it more palatable. Natural man likes the leavened bread. It tastes good. However, we are warned not to do that.

I have confidence in you through the Lord, that ye will be none otherwise minded: but he that troubleth you shall bear his judgment, whosoever he be [Gal. 5:10].

Paul believed that the Galatians would ultimately reject the teaching of the Judaizers. He says, "I have confidence in you" that when you get your feet back on the ground, and your heads out of the clouds, you will return to the gospel that was preached to you, and you will see that the teaching of the Judaizers was an intrusion, that it was leaven.

And I, brethren, if I yet preach circumcision, why do I yet suffer persecution? then is the offence of the cross ceased [Gal. 5:11].

This verse is important to note. Paul asks, "If I preach circumcision, why am I persecuted?" Adding something to the gospel makes it acceptable. The gospel, by itself, is not acceptable to the natural man. Preaching the gospel does antagonize some folk. Paul asks, "If I am including something else in the gospel, why am I being persecuted?"

"Then is the offence of the cross ceased." Actually, the cross of Christ is an offense to all that man prides himself in. It is an offense to his morality because it tells him his work cannot justify him. It is an offense to his philosophy because its appeal is to faith and not to reason. It is an offense to the culture of man because its truths are revealed to babes. It is an offense to his sense of caste because God chooses the poor and humble. It is an offense to his will because it calls for an unconditional surrender. It is an offense to his pride because it shows the exceeding sinfulness of the human heart. And it is an offense to himself because it tells him he must be born again. You know, that was almost insulting to the Pharisee Nicodemus that night when Jesus told him, religious as he was, that he must be born again. For the same reason, a lot of ministers who are preaching the New Birth get in trouble with their congregations. Some members don't want to be born again—they feel like they're good enough as they are. It's an insult to them. The Cross is an offense, but we need to guard against magnifying it.

One of my professors in seminary said a very wise thing. He said, "Young gentlemen, do not tone down the gospel, do not change it, because there is the offense of the Cross. You need to recognize it, but don't *magnify* the offense." Sometimes we become offensive in the way we give the gospel—may the Lord forgive us for doing that. When I was a pastor, a man on my staff antagonized a family and caused them to leave the church. I said to him, "Now look, you and I are not to antagonize people. If anything antagonizes them, let it be the *gospel* I preach—not you or me, but the gospel."

> **I would they were even cut off which trouble you [Gal. 5:12].**

I wish these Judaizers were removed from you.

> **For, brethren, ye have been called unto liberty; only use not liberty for an occasion to the flesh, but by love serve one another [Gal. 5:13].**

There are three methods of trying to live the Christian life—two of them will not work. One is a life of legalism, which Paul has been discussing. The other is the life of license, which Paul discussed in Romans 6: After we are saved by grace, can we live in sin? Paul's answer is, "God forbid." You can't live in sin and be a Christian. Now you may fall into sin, but you will get out of it. The Prodigal Son can get in the pig pen, but he won't settle down there—the pig pen won't be his forwarding address. He will leave it. The Christian life is neither the life of legalism nor the life of license.

The third method of living the Christian life is the life of liberty, and in the remainder of this chapter he will give us the modus operandi for living by liberty. The life of legalism includes not only the Ten Commandments, but a set of regulations that Bible believers follow today. They tell you where you can't go, and what you can't do. I remember a wonderful woman who was a Bible teacher in Texas. She did an outstanding job of teaching the Bible. One day a dear little saint came up to me and asked, "Do you think she is really a Christian? She uses makeup!" Who in the world ever said that makeup was a test of whether or not a person is a Christian? I told this dear saint that the Bible teacher was living under liberty. She might have been using too much makeup, but at her age she probably needed to spread it on a little thicker. Candidly, I do not think it helps her too much, but she has liberty in Christ. Whether you eat meat or do not eat meat won't commend you to God. Whether you use makeup or don't use makeup won't commend you to God. Paul is saying that you can keep every commandment and still not live the Christian life. Even if you kept all Ten Commandments and followed every commandment others put down for you to live by, you still would not be living the Christian life. Also there are the antinomians who think they can do as they please and be living the Christian life. These folk are as extreme as the legalists. The Christian life is not either one; it is liberty in Christ.

"Only use not liberty for an occasion to the flesh." What does the gospel of grace do for the believer? It is grace, not law, that frees us from doing wrong and allows us to do right. Grace does not set us free to sin, but it sets us free from sin. You see, the believer should desire to please God, not because he must please Him like a slave, but because he is a son and he wills to please his Father. He does what God wants, not because he fears to do otherwise like an enemy, but because he wants to do it, for God is his friend. God is the One who loves him. He serves God, not because of pressure from without such as the Law, but because of a great principle within—even the life of Christ that is within him.

We serve God because we *love* Him. The Lord Jesus said to His disciples, "If you love Me, keep My commandments" (see John 14:15). I have often wondered if a disciple had said, "I don't love You," would our Lord have said, "Then forget about My commandments"? The whole basis of obedience is a love relationship to Him. The Law never could bring us to that place. It was negative to begin with. It produced a negative goodness—which is the kind of goodness a great many people have today. Oh, if I could only get this truth through to a great many of the saints! Your negative goodness is a *legal* goodness. You can say, "I don't do this and I don't do that." But what *do* you do? My friend, all legal systems produce only negative goodness. They never rise to the sphere of positive goodness where one does things to please God for the very love of pleasing Him. He wants us to serve Him on that kind of basis.

Now Paul is going to reduce it to a simple statement, then he will amplify what he means.

> **For all the law is fulfilled in one word, even in this;**
> **Thou shalt love thy neighbour as thyself [Gal. 5:14].**

Here the Law is reduced to the lowest common denominator. This is the acid test for those who think they are living by the Law. "Thou shalt love thy neighbour as thyself." The "one word" is *love*.

> **But if ye bite and devour one another, take heed that ye**
> **be not consumed one of another [Gal. 5:15].**

I have always wanted to preach a sermon on this text, and I would entitle it "Christian Cannibals." Did you know that in many churches today the Christians bite, eat, and devour one another? And the bite is as bad as that of a mad dog. There is nothing you can take that will cure the wound. All you can do is suffer. There are a lot of mad dogs running around today. They will bite and devour you. Unfortunately, the world has passed by the church in our day, and I'm sorry it has because there are many fine people in our churches and many wonderful preachers throughout this country. But the lives of some Christians are keeping the world away from certain churches. I personally know examples of this. I know churches in which the Christians have no love for each other, but they bite and devour one another. It is a terrible thing!

SAVED BY FAITH AND WALKING IN THE SPIRIT PRODUCES FRUIT OF THE SPIRIT

Now Paul is going to contrast living in the desires of the flesh with walking in the Spirit. This whole section gives the modus operandi.

As we enter this important section, I want to make a recapitulation and tie it in with what we have had. In this section the theme is sanctification by the Spirit. Paul has told us that we are to "stand fast in the liberty wherewith Christ hath made us free" (v. 1). From what has Christ set us free? Paul has already mentioned several things in this epistle. In chapter 1, verse 4, he tells us that Christ has set us free from this present evil world. That is, we don't have to serve it. Then in chapter 2, verse 20, he says, "I live; yet not I." You and I cannot live the Christian life, but Christ can live it in us. What wonderful liberty! In chapter 3, verse 13, he tells us that we have been delivered from the curse of the Law. We have been delivered from the judgment and the condemnation of the Law. In fact, we have been delivered from the very Law itself: "But when the fulness of the time was come, God sent forth his Son, made of a woman, made under the law, To redeem them that were under the law, that we might receive the adoption of sons" (Gal. 4:4–5).

Now Paul is going to contrast what it is to live in the desires of the flesh with the life of walking in the Spirit. Here is his injunction.

This I say then, Walk in the Spirit, and ye shall not fulfill the lust of the flesh [Gal. 5:16].

This verse states the great principle of Christian living—*walk by means of the Spirit*. The word for *walk* is *peripateō*, which means just "to walk up and down." This Greek word was used for a school of philosophy in Athens, Greece, in which the founder walked up and down as he taught. The principle for us is walking in the Spirit. If we do, we will not "fulfil the lust of the flesh."

The word *lust* in our usage today has an evil connotation, which the Greek word does not have. *Lust* of the flesh refers to the desires of the flesh, many of which are not immoral, but are of the flesh (music, art, and works of dogooders, etc.). There are many things which in themselves are not evil, but they can take the place of spiritual things. Some Christians can get wrapped up in a hobby which takes them away from the Word of God. Many Christians spend a lot of time worshiping before that little idiot box we call TV. Now don't misunderstand—I watch TV. I am not under any law that says I can't watch TV. There are a few programs one can enjoy. But watching TV is a desire of the flesh. If it takes you away from that which is spiritual, then it is wrong.

For the flesh lusteth against the Spirit, and the Spirit against the flesh: and these are contrary the one to the other: so that ye cannot do the things that ye would [Gal. 5:17].

A transliteration of this verse will help convey the meaning: "For the flesh *warreth* against the Spirit, and the Spirit *warreth* against the flesh: and these are contrary the one to the other: so that ye cannot do the things that ye would" that is, the things that the old nature wanted to do. This is very important to see—the flesh wars against the Spirit, and the Spirit wars against the flesh.

A believer has a new nature. This is what our Lord said to Nicodemus when He said, "That which is born of the flesh is flesh; and that which is born of the Spirit is spirit" (John 3:6). The believer still has that old nature of the flesh, and he won't get rid of it in this life. The idea that we can get rid of that old nature is a tragic mistake. John said, "If we say that we have no sin, we deceive ourselves, and the truth is not in us" (1 John 1:8). My friend, if the *truth* is not in you, then you must be a liar. That puts the "perfect" individual in the position of being a liar.

We have two natures—the old and the new. That is what Paul describes in the last part of Romans. He himself experienced the turmoil of two natures, and this has also been the experience of many believers.

The flesh wars against the Spirit, and the Spirit wars against the flesh. Therefore, we cannot do the things that we would like to do. The new nature rebels against the old nature. They are contrary; they are at war with each other. Have you experienced this in your own life?

There is a song we sing entitled "Come Thou Fount by Robert Robinson.

> Come, Thou Fount of every blessing,
> Tune my heart to sing Thy grace;
> Streams of mercy, never ceasing,
> Call for songs of loudest praise.

It is a wonderful hymn. In the last stanza are these words:

> Prone to wander, Lord, I feel it,
> Prone to leave the God I love;

After this song was written, someone looked at it and said, "That is not my experience—I'll change that." So in some hymnbooks we find these words:

> Prone to worship, Lord, I feel it,
> Prone to love the God I serve.

Which is true? Well, both are true. I have a nature that is prone to wander, prone to leave the God I love. There are times when this old nature of mine wants to wander away from the Lord! Have you had this experience? Also I have a new nature that is prone to worship the Lord. There are times when I am riding along alone in my car, and I just cry out to Him, "Oh, Lord, how wonderful You are! I love You and worship You." That is the expression of my new nature; my old nature never gets around to praising Him or loving Him. Every believer has an old and a new nature.

There are folk who say, "Well, I can't tell whether I am walking in the Spirit or not." Don't kid yourself about this. You *can* know. Paul has spelled it out here so that you cannot miss it.

But if ye be led of the Spirit, ye are not under the law [Gal. 5:18].

The Holy Spirit of God brings us to a higher plane.
Now Paul makes clear what the works of the flesh are:

Now the works of the flesh are manifest, which are these; Adultery, fornication, uncleanness, lasciviousness, idolatry, witchcraft, hatred, variance, emulations, wrath, strife, seditions, heresies, envyings, murders, drunkenness, revellings, and such like: of the which I tell you before, as I have also told you in time past, that they which do such things shall not inherit the kingdom of God [Gal. 5:19–21].

This is an ugly brood of sensual sins, religious sins, social sins, and personal sins.

Sensual Sins	Adultery—omitted from the best manuscripts, included in fornication
	Fornication—prostitution
	Uncleanness—(akatharsia) impurity, sexual sins including pornography
	Lasciviousness—brutality, sadism (we see this abounding in our day)
Religious Sins	Idolatry—worship of idols (this includes money and everything that takes the place of God)
	Witchcraft—(pharmakeia) drugs (drugs are used in all heathen religions)
	Hatred—enmity
	Variances—eris (the Greek Eris was the goddess of strife) contentions, quarrels
Social Sins	Emulations—(zelos) rivalry, jealousy
	Wrath—(thumos) a hot temper
	Strife—factions, cliques (little cliques in a church hurt the cause of Christ)

Seditions—divisions
Heresies—parties, sects
Envyings—(phthonos)
Murders—omitted from the best manuscripts
    probably because it is included in other sins
    mentioned here (the Lord said if you hate you
    are guilty of murder)

Personal   Drunkenness
  Sins   Revelings, wantonness

Notice that Paul concludes this list of the works of the flesh by "and such like," which means there are many others he could have mentioned.

"They which do such things shall not inherit the kingdom of God." "Which do" indicates continuous action. Our Lord gave the illustration of the Prodigal Son who got down in the pig pen but didn't stay there. The only ones that stay in a pig pen are pigs. If a son gets there, he will be very unhappy until he gets out. If you can continue to live in sin, you are in a dangerous position. It means you are not a child of God.

Now, having listed the works of the flesh, Paul will list the fruit of the Spirit. Notice the contrast: *works* of the flesh and *fruit* of the Spirit. The works of the flesh are what you do. The Ten Commandments were given to control the flesh. But now the Christian life is to produce the fruit of the Spirit.

But the fruit of the Spirit is love, joy, peace, longsuffering, gentleness, goodness, faith,

Meekness, temperance: against such there is no law [Gal. 5:22–23].

The Lord Jesus Christ talked about the fruit of the Spirit in John 15. He said that without Him we could do nothing. And fruit is what He wants in our lives. He wants fruit, more fruit, and much fruit. In His parable of the sower, He spoke of seed bringing forth thirtyfold, sixtyfold, and an hundredfold (see Matt. 13). He wants us to bear much fruit. Now the fruit is produced by the Lord Jesus using the Spirit of God in our lives. He wants to live His life through us. That is the reason I keep saying that you are never asked to live the Christian life. You are asked to let Him live through you. No believer can live the Christian life himself. The old nature cannot produce the fruit of the Spirit.

Paul makes it clear in Romans 7:18 that the new nature has no *power* to produce the fruit of the Spirit. He said, ". . . to will is present with me; but how to perform that which is good I find not." That is the problem with many of us. How do you do it? This is not a do-it-yourself operation. But how are we going to let the Spirit of God produce the fruit of the Spirit in our lives?

The subject of fruit bearing is an interesting one. When speaking about it, I like to use the illustration of my ranch. I have a ranch in Pasadena. It is not what you would call a big ranch. It is 72 feet wide and goes back about 123 feet. My house is right in the middle of it. I have a nice nectarine tree out in front, which really produces fruit. I have three orange trees, four avocado trees, a lemon tree, and a few other trees. There is never a period during the year in California that I do not have some fruit on some tree. I have observed that fruit is produced by the tree, not by self-effort. As far as I can tell, the branches never get together and say, "Let's all work hard and see what we can do for this fellow, McGee, because he likes fruit." I do enjoy fruit but, as far as I can tell, these branches that bear fruit just open up themselves to the sunshine and to the rain. A bloom appears, then the little green fruit forms, grows, and then ripens.

Another thing that I have noticed is that the limbs never leave the trunk of the tree—they don't get down and run around. Our Lord said, ". . . As the branch cannot bear fruit of itself, except it abide in the vine; no more can ye, except ye abide in me" (John 15:4). Our problem is that we offer ourselves to God as a living sacrifice, but when the altar gets hot, we crawl off. We are to *abide* in Christ if we are to produce fruit.

Paul is stating the principle of fruit-bearing so that we can understand it. The fruit is produced by *yielding*—by yielding to the sweet influences that are about us. I am not talking about the world and neither is Paul. We are to *yield* to the Holy Spirit who indwells us. The

Holy Spirit wants to produce fruit—it is called the fruit of the Spirit.

"The fruit of the Spirit *is* love, joy, peace." Notice it is singular: *is*, not *are*. You can argue about the grammar used here, but it happens to be singular in the Greek. This indicates that love is the fruit, and from it stems all other fruits. Love is primary.

Paul says that without love we ". . . become as sounding brass, or a tinkling cymbal" (1 Cor. 13:1). First Corinthians 13 was never intended to be removed from the Bible, beautifully framed, and hung on the wall. It belongs to the *gifts* of the Spirit, and the gifts are not to be exercised except by the fruit of the Spirit, which is love. You cannot exercise a gift without doing it by the fruit of the Spirit. Love is all-important. Paul continues to say in 1 Corinthians 13 that if you give your body to be burned and give everything that you have, but don't have love, you are a nothing. We need to recognize the importance of what Paul is saying.

Another thing that Paul says in 1 Corinthians 13 is that "love never seeks its own." Love is always doing something for others. A gift is always to be exercised in the church. It is a manifestation of the Spirit to all believers. All believers have a gift and it is to be exercised for the profit of the body of believers. My eyes operate for the benefit of the rest of my body. They guide my body in the right direction. They are important. I cannot imagine my eyes walking out on the rest of my body and saying, "We like looking around, and your feet get tired, so we are going to leave you for awhile." They never do that. We need to recognize that no gift apart from the fruit of the Spirit is to be exercised—and that fruit is love. This is the kind of fruit the Lord Jesus was talking about in John 15. The fruit is the fruit of the Spirit.

"But the fruit of the Spirit is love, joy, peace, longsuffering, gentleness, goodness, faith, meekness, temperance: against such there is no law" (vv. 22–23).

There is "no law" against them, and no law which will produce them. You cannot produce any of these by your own effort. Have you ever tried being meek, for instance? If you tried being meek, and accomplished it, you would be proud that you became meek, and then you would lose your meekness and humility.

For a moment let us look at the fruit of the Spirit. It should characterize the lives of believers. I used to hear the late Dr. Jim McGinley say, "I am not to judge you, but I am a fruit inspector, and I have a right to look at the fruit you are producing." The question is, are you producing any fruit in your life?

Now love ought to be in your heart and life if you are a believer. But, friend, if there are sensual sins in your life, you will never know what real love is. There are many young people today who know a great deal about sex, but they know nothing about love. Love is a fruit of the Spirit, and God will give this love to a husband for his wife, and to the wife for her husband. I don't think anyone can love like two Christians can love. My, how they can love each other!

I shall never forget the night I proposed to my wife. She did not accept me that night, but when she did, we had prayer and dedicated our lives to the Lord. I told her, "I am a preacher who speaks out plainly. I may get into trouble some day. We may find ourselves out on the street." I shall never forget what she said to me: "Well, I'll just beat the drum for you if you have to get out on the street!" That is love on a higher plane.

When we lost our first little girl, I did not want the doctor to tell my wife—I wanted to tell her. When I gave her the news, we wept together and then we prayed. Love like that is the fruit of the Holy Spirit.

Joy is a fruit that the Lord Jesus wants you to have in your life. He came that we might have joy—that we might have fun. I wish we had more fun times in our churches today. The world has what they call the "happy hour" in cocktail parlors all across our land. People don't look too happy when they go in, and they sure don't look happy when they come out! They are a bunch of sots, if you please. That's not joy. John says, "And these things write we unto you, that your joy may be full" (1 John 1:4). These things were written that you might really enjoy life. Are you really living it up today, friend? I hope you are as a believer.

The third fruit is peace, the peace of God. Religion can never give this to you. Only Christ can give you deep-down peace—". . . being justified by faith, we have peace with God through our Lord Jesus Christ" (Rom. 5:1).

There are some other fruits. Are you longsuffering—that is, patient and long tempered? This is an area where I need some help, and only the Spirit of God can do it. I found out that I cannot do it.

Then there is the fruit of gentleness, which means kindness; there is goodness, which means kind but firm.

Faith, in this list, means faithfulness. If you are a child of God, you will be faithful. If you are married, you will be faithful to your husband or wife. If you are an employee, you are going to be faithful to your job and to your boss. If you are a church member, you are going to be faithful to your church. You are going to be faithful wherever you are and in whatever you do.

Next comes meekness, and that does not mean mildness. Two men who were truly meek were Moses and the Lord Jesus Christ. Perhaps you don't think Moses was meek when he came down from the Mount, found the people were worshiping a golden calf, and administered disciplinary judgment (see Exod. 32). But he was meek. Was Jesus meek when He ran the money-changers out of the temple? Meekness is not mildness and it is not weakness. Meekness means that you will do God's will, that you are willing to yield your will to the will of God. Finally, there is temperance, which is self-control—Christian poise is so needed today.

And they that are Christ's have crucified the flesh with the affections and lusts [Gal. 5:24].

When was the flesh crucified? When they reckon that when Christ died, they died, they will yield themselves on that basis. In Romans 6:13 Paul says, "Neither yield ye your members as instruments of unrighteousness unto sin: but yield yourself unto God, as those that are alive from the dead, and your members as instruments of righteousness unto God."

"For ye are dead, and your life is hid with Christ in God" (Col. 3:3). "I am crucified with Christ: nevertheless I live; yet not I, but Christ liveth in me: and the life which I now live in the flesh I live by the faith of the Son of God, who loved me, and gave himself for me" (Gal. 2:20). In all of these passages the thought is that when Christ was crucified, the believer was crucified at the same time. The believer is now joined to the living Christ, and the victory is not by struggling but by surrendering to Christ. The scriptural word is *yield;* it is an act of the will.

This is the key to it all:

If we live in the Spirit, let us also walk in the Spirit [Gal. 5:25].

A professor in a theological seminary called my attention to the word *walk* in this verse several years ago, and it has meant a great deal to me. As you recall, back in verse 16 a "*walk* in the Spirit" is *parapateō*, but here "walk" is a different Greek word. It is *stoichomen,* which is basic and elemental, meaning "to proceed or step in order." In verse 16 we were given the principle of walk; here in verse 25 it means to learn to walk. Just as we learned to walk physically by the trial and error method, so are we to begin to walk by the Spirit—it is a learning process.

Let me illustrate this principle with a ridiculous illustration. What is walking? Walking is putting one foot in front of the other. You may have heard about the knock-kneed girl. One knee said to the other, "If you let me by this time, I will let you by next time." That is walking, putting one foot in front of the other. This means to learn to walk. How did you learn to walk? Were you given a lecture on the subject? Did you go to a school and take a course in learning to walk? One summer my grandson, who was about twelve months old at the time, stayed with us for a time. He was just standing and wobbling along. I did not put him in his high chair and tell him about the physical mechanism of the foot. I did not give him a lecture on the psychology of walking or the sociological implications of walking. If I had explained all of these things to my grandson, could he have lifted the tray of his high chair and walked off? No, my friend, that is not the way you learn to walk. You learn to walk by trial and error. One time my grandson fell down hard, and he had a big knot on his forehead. He fell many times, but before long he was walking and running and climbing as surefootedly as a mountain goat. He learned to do it by just *doing* it, by trial and error.

This is the way we are to learn to walk in the Spirit—by trial and error. I know people who have attended Keswick conferences, spiritual life conferences, and Bible conferences; they have their notebooks filled with notes on how to live the Christian life. Still they are not living it. What is the problem?

You have to *learn* to walk in the Spirit, which means you are to start out. Why not start now? Say, "I am going to walk in the Spirit. I am going to depend upon the Holy Spirit to produce the fruits in my life." Perhaps you are thinking that you might fall down. I have news for you—you are going to fall. It will hurt. You say, "How many times will I fall?" I don't know. I am still falling. But that is the way you are going to walk in the Spirit, and that's the only way. My friend, you need to step out today and begin leaning upon the Spirit of God. Yield yourself to Him; it is an act of the will.

Every day I start my day by saying, "Lord, I can't live today in a way that pleases You, and I want You to do it through me." I find there are times when I don't get but a few blocks from home when something happens. One morning a woman in a Volkswagen cut in front of me. I had been so nice and sweet up to then, but I drove up beside her car and I told her what she had done. And she told me a thing or two right back. When she drove off, I thought, *My, I sure fell on my face!* When I do that, I just get up and start over again.

Let us not be desirous of vain glory, provoking one another, envying one another [Gal. 5:26].

"Let us not be desirous of vain glory"—you and I are *never* going to be wonderful saints of God. *He* is wonderful. Oh, how wonderful He is! He is worthy of our worship. Let's start walking, depending on Him like little children. That's what He wants us to do.

"Provoking one another" is challenging one another. We are not to challenge and envy one another. We are to get down from our high chairs and start walking in the Spirit. The Christian life is not a balloon ascension with some great overpowering experience of soaring to the heights. Rather it is a daily walk; it is a matter of putting one foot ahead of the other, in dependence upon the Holy Spirit.

CHAPTER 6

THEME: Saved by faith and fruit of the Spirit presents Christian character; autographed conclusion; Paul's testimony

This final chapter of Galatians brings us to the third step in this practical section of sanctification by the Spirit. We have seen that being saved by faith and living by law perpetrates falling from grace. Also we have seen that being saved by faith and walking in the Spirit produces fruit of the Spirit. In other words, we have seen what it means to walk in the Spirit. It is something we are to begin, and though we fail, we are to keep at it. Now we will see how the fruit of the Spirit will work out in our lives. Here is where we see it put in shoe leather where it can hit the pavement of our hometown.

SAVED BY FAITH AND FRUIT OF THE SPIRIT PRESENTS CHRISTIAN CHARACTER

Brethren, if a man be overtaken in a fault, ye which are spiritual, restore such an one in the spirit of meekness; considering thyself, lest thou also be tempted [Gal. 6:1].

Who is the "man" mentioned in this verse? It is a generic term and refers to any man or woman who is a Christian. The word *fault*, taken from the Greek *paraptōma*, means "a falling aside or mishap." It means "to stumble." It may not refer to a great sin but to an awful blunder.

Now what is to be done to a person who is overtaken in a fault? Well, the "spiritual" folk, and many think they are spiritual, interpret this as meaning they are to beat him on the head with a baseball bat because he has done something wrong. There is a danger of not really wanting to restore him. We would much rather criticize and condemn him. However, the believer does not lose his salvation when he sins. If a Christian is overtaken in a fault, a spiritual Christian is to restore that one in the spirit of meekness. Meekness is one of the fruits of the Spirit.

The word used for "fault" in this verse is the same word used to describe the Lord Jesus Christ in the Garden of Gethsemane when He fell on His face and prayed (see Matt. 26:39). It means "to stumble." If a man be overtaken in a fault, he stumbles. He may commit a small sin or an awful blunder.

One of the wonderful things said about the Lord Jesus in prophecy is found in Isaiah 63:9, "In all their affliction he was afflicted, and the angel of his presence saved them: in his love and in his pity he redeemed them; and he bare them, and carried them all the days of old." Now the better manuscripts say, "In all their affliction He was not afflicted." I like that much better. The Lord Jesus goes along with me through life, and when I stumble and fall down, He does not fall. He is not afflicted. He is there beside me and He picks me up, brushes me off, and tells me to start out again. It is a comforting thing to know that I have One near me who is not afflicted in my affliction.

The word used for "restore" in this verse is a verb which means "to set a broken bone." If a fellow falls down and breaks his leg, what are you going to do? Are you going to walk off and leave him in pain? God says, "You who are spiritual set the broken bone. Get him back on his feet again." It is to be done in the spirit of meekness.

One of the great preachers of the South was marvelously converted when he was a drunkard. His ministry was quite demanding and after a great deal of pressure and temptation he got drunk one night. He was so ashamed that the very next day he called in his board of deacons and turned in his resignation. He told them, "I want to resign." They were amazed. They asked why. He frankly told them, "I got drunk last night. A preacher should not get drunk, and I want to resign." It was obvious that he was ashamed, and do you know what those wonderful deacons did? They put their arms around him and said, "Let's all pray." They would not accept his resignation. A man who was present in the congregation that next Sunday said, "I never heard a greater sermon in my life than that man preached." Those deacons were real surgeons—they set a broken bone; they restored him.

There are some people who would have put him out of the ministry, but these deacons put that preacher back on his feet, and God marvelously used him after that.

"Ye which are spiritual, restore such an one in the spirit of meekness." Notice that you are to restore him in the spirit of meekness. A spiritual man will have the fruit of the Spirit in his life: love, joy, peace, longsuffering, gentleness, goodness, faithfulness, and meekness. You are to restore him in meekness.

"Considering thyself, lest thou also be tempted." Don't think that you are immune to what you are pointing your finger and blaming another brother for doing. You could do the same thing. So restore him in the spirit of meekness.

Bear ye one another's burdens, and so fulfil the law of Christ [Gal. 6:2].

This is a verse that caused me as a boy to wonder about the accuracy of the Bible.

Most little towns of a bygone day had a character known as the town atheist, a free-thinker, generally a ne'er-do-well, although sometimes he was one of the leading citizens of the community. The little town in which I lived as a boy lacked many things. It didn't have street lights. In fact, we didn't have electric lights in our home, and I can remember using the lamp to study by in those days. Our little town didn't have sidewalks; it didn't have paved streets. It didn't have running water—except what you ran out to the well to get; and we didn't have inside plumbing. There were many things our little town lacked, but we did have a town atheist. He called himself a socialist. Each Sunday morning, weather permitting, he was down at the street corner on the town square, speaking. Generally he had about a dozen listeners, who were also loafers. On my way to Sunday school—I killed as much time as possible—I always stopped to listen to him. The thing that impressed me about this atheist was that his mouth was cut on a bias, and as he chewed tobacco an amazing thing took place. He not only defied the Word of God, he also defied the law of gravitation. You would think, according to the law of gravitation, that the tobacco juice would run out of the lower corner of his mouth. But it didn't. It ran out of the upper corner. I used to stand there as a boy and wonder how he did it.

This man, I remember, always ridiculed the Bible, and he pointed out supposed contradictions. His favorites were these two verses in the sixth chapter of Galatians: "Bear ye one another's burdens, and so fulfil the law of Christ" (v. 2). Then he would read, "For every man shall bear his own burden" (v. 5). He would read both verses, then lift his head and leer at the crowd and say, "You see, there is a contradiction in the Bible. One place it says that you're to bear one another's burdens, and then it says you are to bear your own burdens." None of us in the little town knew how to answer him, so we just stood there with our mouths open and listened to him. Actually, the answer was very simple, but we didn't know it in those days.

There are in the Scriptures eleven different words that are translated by our one English word burden. This means there are different kinds of burdens. There are some burdens that you can share; there are burdens that you must bear and you cannot share them with anyone. That is a very simple but a very satisfactory answer.

Now burdens are those things that we all have in common. All of us have burdens. Not all of us have wealth, but we have burdens. Not all of us have health, but we have burdens. Not all of us have talents, but we have burdens. Some of us lack even physical members—not all of us can see, not all of us can hear, not all of us have arms and legs, and certainly not all of us have good looks. We say that we all have the same blood, but it is not the same; it comes in different types. We do not have very much in common, but we all have burdens.

There is a Spanish proverb that goes something like this: "No home is there anywhere that does not sooner or later have its hush." Also the French have a proverb: "Everyone thinks his own burden is heaviest." A woman in Southern California who has done a great deal of work with children said, "Even children have burdens." Burdens are common to the human family. We all have burdens.

However not all of us have the same burdens. We have many different burdens. What Paul is doing in this sixth chapter of Galatians is dividing burdens into two classes: burdens which we can share, and burdens which we must bear, and cannot share. Those of us in our little town didn't know there were two different words used in the Greek. In verse 2 you could translate it like this: "The burdens of each other, keep bearing." The Greek word for burden is *baros*, meaning "something heavy." Our Lord used it when He spoke about the burden and the heat of the day (see Matt. 20:12). And for the early church, when it met in its first council in Jerusalem, made this decision: "For it seemed good to the Holy Spirit and to us, to lay upon you no greater burden than these necessary things" (Acts 15:28, italics mine), speaking of a burden they were to share with the church in Jerusalem. Someone has said that a load is only half a load when two are carrying it. There are burdens today that we can share.

A woman boarded a bus with a very heavy basket. She sat down beside a man and put the basket on her lap. After noticing her discomfort he said, "Lady, if you would put that heavy basket down on the floor you would find that the bus would carry both you and your load!" May I say to you, there are burdens that you can let someone else bear with you.

Now burden (*baros*) means "fault"—"If a man be overtaken in a fault." That's his burden. You could help him bear it. It also means infirmity, a weakness, an ignorance, a pressure, a tension, a grief.

I think everybody has a fault. A man speaking to a group asked the question, "Is there anyone here who does not have a fault, or do you know someone who does not have a fault?" No one raised his hand. After he had repeated the question several times, a little fellow in the back, a Mr. Milquetoast type, raised his hand. The speaker asked him to stand. "Are you the one who has no faults?" "Oh, no," he said, "I'm not the one." "Then do you know someone who does not have any faults?" "Well," he said, "I don't exactly know him, but I have heard of him." The man who was lecturing said, "Tell me, who is he?" The little fellow said, "He's my wife's first husband." And I have a notion that he had heard of him quite a few times, by the way.

All of us have faults, and that's a burden. Many times we fall down, and many times we see a brother fall down. "Ye which are spiritual, restore such an one."

Then there is another burden that you and I can share: tensions.

Now you can take a tranquilizer, but, my friend, that really won't solve your problems. We are living today in a time of tension such as the human family has never before experienced. I don't know about you, but I live in "Tension Town." Many of us in these great metropolitan areas are under pressure and tension today. This is certainly a burden we need to bear with one another.

Let me illustrate. A very dear man, in one of the churches I pastored, came to me and said, "Do you have something against me?" "No, I said, "why do you say that?" "Well, I met you down on the street and you didn't even speak to me." I was amazed. "I didn't?" "No. You just passed me right by. You looked right at me." I said, "I didn't see you." "You must have—you looked right at me." So I asked him what day that was, and realized it was the day the airlines got my tickets mixed up, and I was going down there to straighten them out. My friend, we are under tension at a time like that. And my friend was also under tension for assuming I had snubbed him. Well, I never shall forget, he put his arm around me and said, "I'm glad to know that." You see, he was helping me bear the burden of tension. That's something we can share with each other.

Now I come to the third burden you and I can share. That is the burden known as grief. The burden of tragedy, the burden of sorrow, the burden of disappointment is inevitable in the human family. If it hasn't come to you, it will come. And when it comes we need somebody, a friend, to stand with us. The three friends of Job—we criticize them because they began a talking marathon, but actually they first spent seven days sitting with Job and sorrowing with him.

In a book of natural history there is a statement that reads: "Man is the only one that knows nothing, and that can learn nothing without being taught. He can neither speak, nor walk, nor eat. In short, he can do nothing at the prompting of nature but weep." All that you and I know to do when we come into this world is weep. We come into this world with a cry, and we need comfort. From the very beginning and all through life we need comfort because of the fact that we have been born into this world of woe.

Ruth could say to Boaz, "Thou hast comforted me" (see Ruth 2:13). She was a stranger, an outcast, who had come from a foreign country and expected to be kept on the outside, but into her life came someone who showed an interest in her and extended to her certain courtesies. With appreciation she said, "Thou hast comforted me."

Mary broke an alabaster box of ointment upon our Lord. She did this shortly before His crucifixion because she knew what was going to take place. No one else seemed to realize what was happening, but she knew. Jesus said, "Let her alone; for the day of my burial hath she kept this" (see Matt. 26:12). She alone entered into His sufferings. And He said, "Verily I say unto you, Wheresoever this gospel shall be preached in the whole world, there shall also this, that this woman hath done, be told for a memorial of her" (Matt. 26:13). And the fragrance of that ointment has filled the world. Grief is a burden that you can share. There will be those who will come to you in your sorrow.

Our faults, our tensions, our griefs are some of the burdens that you and I can share.

> Is thy cruse of comfort failing?
>   Raise and share it with a friend,
> And thro' all the years of famine
>   It shall serve thee to the end.
>
> Love Divine will fill thy storehouse,
>   Or thy handful still renew;
> Scanty fare for one will often
>   Make a royal feast for two.
>
> Lost and weary on the mountains,
>   Wouldst thou sleep amidst the snow?
> Chafe that frozen form beside thee,
>   And together both shall glow.
>
> Art thou wounded in life's battle?
>   Many stricken round thee moan;
> Give to them thy precious ointment,
>   And that balm shall heal thine own.
>   —Author unknown

There are burdens that we can share.

Now let's look at the other verse that tells us there are burdens which we cannot share.

But let every man prove his own work, and then shall he have rejoicing in himself alone, and not in another [Gal. 6:4].

I think he means that we are not to run around getting everybody to carry our burdens.

For every man shall bear his own burden [Gal. 6:5].

The word *burden* here is the Greek *phortion*, meaning "a load to be borne." This word is used to speak of a ship's cargo. Actually, it is used to speak of a child in the womb—only the mother could bear it, you see. This is a load that is impossible to share. While I never recommend J. B. Phillips' *New Testament in Modern English* as a translation (it should not be called a translation), it is a most excellent explanation. Many times it throws light on a passage of Scripture. He gives this paraphrase of Galatians 6:5: "For every man must 'shoulder his own pack.'" That's it. Each man must shoulder his own pack. There is an old bromide: "To every man his work." And another, a rather crude one, "Every tub must sit on its own bottom." In other words, there are burdens today that you and I cannot share.

Every life, in one sense, is separated, it is isolated, it is segregated, it is quarantined from every other life. Dr. Funk, of the *Funk and Wagnalls Dictionary*, has compiled a list of words in which the saddest word in the English language is *alone*. There are certain burdens that you and I will have to bear alone. I will mention just a few of them here—you will think of others.

The first one I want to mention is suffering. You will have to suffer alone. No one can suffer for you. You are born into this world alone— and it's a world of woe; you will suffer alone. You will have to face certain problems alone. There will be physical suffering that will come to you. You will get sick, and no one can take your place.

When my daughter was a very little thing, we were coming back from Texas, and she started running a high fever. We took her to the hospital in Globe, Arizona. A doctor gave her certain medication and told us, "You give her this and the fever will go down. It is getting late in the afternoon so keep driving to California and get out of this heat." So we started out. In Phoenix we stopped for gasoline, and my wife took her temperature. It registered 104°—her temperature hadn't gone down. We were frightened. We went to a motel, called a doctor, and told him the situation. He said to continue the medication and to bring her to the hospital in the morning. Never shall I forget my feelings as I carried her to the hospital and laid her down. Never in my life had I had that experience. I would have gladly taken that fever in my own body—*gladly* would I have done it. But, my friend, I could not do it. We have to suffer alone. You cannot get someone to substitute for you. Suffering is one thing that we cannot share. Mental anguish is another type of suffering that you cannot share. Oh, the number of folk who are disappointed. They are even bitter today because of some great disappointment. Suffering is a burden that we have to bear alone.

There is another burden that you and I cannot share with anyone else. It is death. We cannot share this with another. There will come a time when each of us will go down through the valley of the shadow of death, and we will go alone. Thomas Hobbes, an agnostic all of his life, a very brilliant man, said when he came to his death, "I am taking a fearful leap into the dark!" And then he cried out, "Oh, God, it is lonely!" Yes, it is. Death is a burden you cannot share. John Haye, at one time Secretary of State, was quite a writer. He wrote a poem portraying death entitled "The Stirrup Cup," having in mind the cavalrymen who used to drink when they mounted their steeds. This is the way he began:

> My short and happy day is done,
> The long and lonely night comes on:
> And at my door the pale horse stands
> To bear me forth to unknown lands.

And, my friend, when death comes, you and I will be riding alone. Death is a burden that you will have to bear alone.

We come now to the third and last burden that I shall mention. It bears an unusual name, by the way. It is the *Bēma*. The *Bēma* is the judgment seat of Christ. It is not for the unsaved; it is for Christians. Oh, yes, there is a judgment for the unbeliever, the Great White Throne Judgment described in the twentieth chapter of Revelation. But the *Bēma Seat* is for the Christian. "For we must all appear before the judgment seat of Christ; that every one may receive the things done in his body, according to that he hath done, whether it be good or bad" (2 Cor. 5:10). Everything that we have done in the flesh as a Christian is to be judged to see whether or not we receive a reward. Salvation is not in question—that was settled for the believer at the cross of Christ. It is the works of the believer that are to be judged at the *Bēma Seat*. "So then every one of us shall give account of himself to God" (Rom. 14:12).

Then Paul puts down a principle which is applicable to every avenue of life but is specifically given to believers: "Be not deceived; God is not mocked: for whatsoever a man soweth, that shall he also reap" (v. 7). This principle is true in the realm of nature. You sow cotton; you reap cotton. You sow wheat; you reap wheat. And as a Christian you will reap what you sow. We like to sing "The Old Account Was Settled Long Ago." In a believer's life this is true—but what about the new account? What about the account since you were saved? What has your life been since you accepted Christ? Do you have sin in your life? Have you confessed it? We are all to appear before the judgment seat of Christ. "But if we walk in the light, as he is in the light, we have fellowship one with another, and the blood of Jesus Christ his Son cleanseth us from all sin" (1 John 1:7).

Somebody will say, "I'm a Christian. I don't have any sin." You don't? Then you are not in the light. If you will get in the light you will see the sin that is in your life. The light—which is the Word of God—reveals what is there. Try this one on for size: "Therefore to him that knoweth to do good, and doeth it not, to him it is sin" (James 4:17). Does that fit you today? I think it will fit all of us. He that knows to do good, and does it not, sins. Your life as a child of God is a burden that you carry, and you will have to bring it before Him some day.

Now there is another type of burden which you can neither bear nor share. It is a burden the Scriptures speak of: the burden of sin. Paul speaks of it in the first part of Romans. David in the Psalms says: "For mine iniquities are gone over mine head: as an heavy burden they are too heavy for me" (Ps. 38:4). Sin is a burden you cannot share with anyone else. And sin is a burden you cannot bear, my friend. "My iniquities," David says, "are gone over my head: as an heavy burden they are too heavy for me." Also from the Psalms comes this longing: "And I said, Oh that I had wings like a dove! for then would I fly away, and be at rest" (Ps. 55:6). Have you ever felt like that? Sometimes the doctor recommends that we get away from it all. The psalmist says, "If I could only run away from it." But you and I cannot run away from it because we have a guilt complex. A psychologist out here at the University of Southern California tells me that the guilt complex is as much a part of us as our right arm. The psychologists have tried to get rid of it. They have not succeeded. Everyone has it. Sir Arthur Conan Doyle, the writer of detective stories and creator of Sherlock Holmes, liked to play practical jokes. At one time he sent a telegram to twelve famous people in London whom he knew. The telegram read, "Flee at once. All is discovered." All twelve of them left the country—yet all of them were upright citizens. May I say to you, my beloved, we all have a guilt complex. Sin is that burden which we can neither share nor bear. It is too heavy for us.

There is only one place you can get rid of it, and that is at the cross of Christ. "Cast thy burden upon the LORD, and he shall sustain thee: he shall never suffer the righteous to be moved" (Ps. 55:22). The Lord Jesus said "Come unto me, all ye that labour and are heavy laden, and I will give you rest" (Matt. 11:28). He alone can lift the heavy burden of sin today, and it is because He paid the penalty for it. He alone can lift it; He alone can take it from you.

There are two famous pieces of sculpture that depict this. One is "The Dying Gaul" and the other is "The Laocöon," which is in Rome at the Vatican. "The Dying Gaul" depicts a man who has been brought down as a captive and slave to Rome, then put into the arena as a gladiator and mortally wounded. He is lying there, his life blood flowing from him, and he is looking up for help. He is in a strange land, and there is nobody, nobody there to help him. A dying gladiator. May

I say to you that this is a picture of any man today without Christ. Christ alone can help us, for that is the reason He came into the world. He said: "For the Son of man is come to seek and to save that which was lost" (Luke 19:10). He also said: ". . . The Son of man came not to be ministered unto, but to minister, and to give his life a ransom for many" (Mark 10:45). Christ paid the penalty for your sin and my sin. Like the dying gladiator, we can look to Him and be saved.

The other piece of sculpture is "The Laocöon." A priest of Troy looked out and saw two sea serpents come and coil themselves about his two sons. He went to their aid, but he could not help them because the sea serpents also enmeshed him in their coils. There they are—all three of them going down to death. To me this illustrates the fact that personal sin is a burden that we cannot cope with. It will take us down to death—eternal death.

What do you do with your burdens?

There are some burdens that you can share. There are others that you must bear alone. But the burden of personal sin is a burden too heavy for you; it is the burden you cannot bear. Over nineteen hundred years ago Christ took the burden of your sin, and He bore it on the cross. Today your burden is either on you, or by faith you have received Christ as your Savior and it is on Him. It cannot be both places—your sin is either on you or it is on Christ. And Christ does not *share* it—He bore it all.

Let him that is taught in the word communicate unto him that teacheth in all good things [Gal. 6:6].

This is probably the bluntest verse in the Bible. Paul is really putting it on the line. The Greek word koinōneō, translated "communicate," means sharing, taking part—sharing the things of Christ together. Paul is bluntly saying this: "Pay your preacher. If someone ministers to your spiritual benefits, minister to him with material benefits." If God has blessed you materially and you are being blessed by someone spiritually, then you ought to minister to that person with material benefits. This is put on a grace basis of sharing, but believe me, friend, if you go into a grocery store and buy bread and meat and go by the checkout stand without paying for it, you are in trouble. There are many people who are ministered to spiritually, but when they go by the checkout counter, they don't share. No one thinks anything about it. The Word of God says that you are to share with those who minister to you.

Be not deceived; God is not mocked: for whatsoever a man soweth, that shall he also reap [Gal. 6:7].

This is one of those remarkable verses in Scripture. This is an immutable law that operates in every sphere of life. In agriculture and horticulture if you sow corn, you get corn; if you sow cotton, you reap cotton. In the moral sphere you also reap what you sow. In the Book of Matthew, chapter 13, the Lord Jesus Christ told about a sower that went forth to sow. He also told us about a reaper that went forth to reap.

One day a visitor in a penitentiary passed by a cell where a man was patching his prison garb with needle and thread. The visitor, wanting to begin a conversation with the prisoner, said, "What are you doing? Sewing? The prisoner looked up and replied, "No, reaping!" That is the point of this verse. The principle stated here is immutable, invariable, unalterable, and cannot be revoked. It cannot be changed one iota, and it is applicable to every sphere and field of life. When you sow wheat, you will get wheat. You will never pick a squash off of a walnut tree. Sometimes a watermelon vine extends out twenty feet in one direction, but it has never been known to make the mistake of putting a pumpkin on the end of it. It always puts a watermelon out there. There is wheat being found in tombs in Egypt that was put there five thousand years ago. They planted it and it came up wheat. In five thousand years the seed did not forget that it was wheat. What you sow you will reap and that will never change.

There are many men in the Bible who illustrate this principle. One of them is Jacob, whose story is told in Genesis 27—29. Jacob deceived his father, Isaac. He put on a goatskin and pretended to be his brother Esau, who was a hairy outdoorsman, in order to receive the blessing given to the oldest son. After deceiving his father, Jacob ran away and lived with his Uncle Laban for several years. He thought he had gotten away with deceiving his father. But remember, God says that what you sow you will reap. You won't reap something similar; you will reap the identical thing that you sow. What happened to Jacob? He fell in love with Rachel, Laban's youngest daughter. He served seven years for her. They had the wedding, and when he lifted the veil, what did he have? He did not have Rachel, the younger daughter; he had Leah, the older daughter. I have a notion that Jacob learned a real lesson on his honeymoon. He had deceived his father by pretending to be the older son when he was actually the younger son. Now his uncle gave him the older daughter when he thought he was getting the younger daughter. Believe me, chickens do come home to roost!

In 1 Kings 21 we find the story of Ahab and Jezebel and their murderous plot to take Naboth's vineyard. Ahab coveted Naboth's vineyard, but Naboth did not want to sell his land. But since Ahab and Jezebel were king and queen, they usually took what they wanted. Jezebel had Naboth killed and Ahab took possession of the vineyard. They thought they would get away with their evil deed, but God sent Elijah to them with a message: ". . . Thus saith the LORD, In the place where dogs licked the blood of Naboth shall dogs lick thy blood, even thine" (1 Kings 21:19). Later Ahab was wounded in battle. He told his chariot driver to take him out of the battle, and the blood from his wound ran out into his chariot. After the battle, he was brought back to Samaria, and there in the pool of Samaria they washed the chariot, and the dogs licked up the blood.

Another example is the apostle Paul. He was a leader in the stoning of Stephen, and after his conversion, when he was over in the Galatian country, he was stoned. You may think that, because he was converted and his sins were forgiven, he would not reap what he had sown. But it is a law of God that "whatsoever a man soweth, that shall he also reap."

I remember well hearing Mel Trotter, the evangelist who was a drunkard before his conversion. I had invited him to Nashville, Tennessee, to hold evangelistic meetings. One night after a meeting we went to a place called Candyland and everybody ordered a great big sloppy banana split, or a milkshake, or a malt. All Mel Trotter ordered was a little bitty glass of carbonated water. Everyone began to rib him about it, and asked him the reason. I shall never forget his answer, "When the Lord gave me a new heart at my conversion, He did not give me a new stomach. I am paying for the years I spent drinking." May I say again, "Whatsoever a man soweth, that shall he also reap." Don't be deceived. God is not mocked. You won't get by with it.

I wish young people would realize the truth of this principle. Many of them are taking drugs. Many are trying to satisfy themselves by indulging in easy sex, free love. Some of them are already beginning to reap the results of what they have sown. Venereal disease has reached epidemic proportions in many states in America, and there is an alarming rise in mental disorders. Why? God says that you will not get by with sin—regardless of how many pills you take. God says you will reap what you sow. God will not be mocked. When you sow corn, you reap corn. When you sow sin, that is what you will reap. Someone may say, "I got converted." That is wonderful, but you are still going to have a payday someday. You will still reap what you have sown.

> **For he that soweth to his flesh shall of the flesh reap corruption; but he that soweth to the Spirit shall of the Spirit reap life everlasting [Gal. 6:8].**

Reaping "life everlasting" includes the fruit of the Spirit in this life and the glorious prospect of the future.

I think many Christians really ought to be fearful of the return of Christ for His own, because it is then that we shall go before the judgment seat of Christ to give an account of the things done in the flesh. My friend, you may be saved, but it may still be very embarrassing for you in that day when you give an account of your life to Him. John mentions the fact that it is possible to be ashamed at His appearing (see 1 John 2:28). If you are going to live in the flesh, you will produce the things of the flesh. That does not, however, mean that you will lose your salvation, but it does mean that you will lose your reward, which will make it a day of shame and regret when you stand before Him.

God has put up a red light; now He puts up a green light. Here are words for your comfort and encouragement.

And let us not be weary in well-doing: for in due season we shall reap, if we faint not [Gal. 6:9].

A father said to me some time ago, "I'm concerned about my boys." He is a doctor, and he said, "The tide is against me. The schools are against me. Other parents seem to be against me, and even some friends are against me. But I want to raise my boys right." If that is your concern, my friend, let me encourage you to sow the right seed. Be patient, and you will reap what you have sown. In Kansas you can't go out and cut grain in January. You have to wait until the time of reaping comes. So just keep sowing. You may have problems and difficulties today, but just keep sowing the Word of God. The Lord has promised: "For as the rain cometh down, and the snow from heaven, and returneth not thither, but watereth the earth, and maketh it bring forth and bud, that it may give seed to the sower, and bread to the eater: So shall my word be that goeth forth out of my mouth: it shall not return unto me void, but it shall accomplish that which I please, and it shall prosper in the thing whereto I sent it" (Isa. 55:10–11).

Remember that Abraham believed God and walked with Him in the land of Canaan. At that time the Canaanite—wicked and idolatrous—was in the land. A son, Isaac, was born to Abraham. When Isaac became a young man, Abraham took him to the top of Mount Moriah. In obedience to God's command, Abraham prepared to offer his son as a sacrifice. God, however, did not let him go through with it. Abraham sowed to the Spirit and he reaped life everlasting.

Jochebed was the mother of Moses. Because of the terrible times in which they lived, she devised a plan to save his life, and he was adopted by Pharaoh's daughter. By God's wonderful arrangement, Jochebed was able to be his nursemaid while he was young. Undoubtedly she taught Moses about God and His call to Abraham and about His purpose for Israel. Then she saw her boy grow up like an Egyptian. All Egypt was against her—the culture of Egypt, the pleasures of Egypt, the philosophy of Egypt, and the religion of Egypt. But there came a day when Moses forsook the pleasures and sins of Egypt and went out to take his place with God's people. Jochebed reaped what she had sown.

We also have an illustration of this principle in the life of David. His sin was glaring, and many folk think of him as being a cruel, sinful man. But sin did not characterize David's life. It is interesting that a drop of black ink on a white tablecloth can be seen from a long distance, but a drop of black ink on a black suit would never be noticed. Other kings during that period of time were so bad that, when they committed a sin such as David did, it would not be noticed. But in David's life it stands out like a horrible blot. David had a heart for God. Even in his confession, he reveals his hunger and thirst for God. But David sowed sin and reaped a terrible harvest in the lives of his own children.

We reap what we sow, my friend. "And let us not be weary in well-doing: for in due season we shall reap, if we faint not."

As we have therefore opportunity, let us do good unto all men, especially unto them who are of the household of faith [Gal. 6:10].

Now Paul moves on. He says that we ought to be do-gooders. Now I recognize that the entire religion of liberalism is one of "doing good." I believe in doing good, but you have to have the right foundation under the good deeds. The right foundation is the gospel of the grace of God and walking in the Spirit of God. When you walk in the Spirit, the fruit of the Spirit is produced. Then, my friend, you are going to do good. You will do good for all men, especially for other believers.

AUTOGRAPHED CONCLUSION

This brings us to the last major division of the epistle to the Galatians. Three handwritings are mentioned in this final section. The first is Paul's own handwriting.

Ye see how large a letter I have written unto you with mine own hand [Gal. 6:11].

"How large a letter" doesn't mean a long letter. This Epistle to the Galatians is only six chapters, while his Epistle to the Romans (which deals with practically the same subject) is sixteen chapters. This could not be called a long letter. But Paul is saying that he has written with large letters, which is characteristic with folk who have poor vision. This, I believe, bears out the theory that Paul's "thorn in the flesh" was eye trouble (see 2 Cor. 12:7). As you recall, he had said to them earlier, ". . . I bear you record, that, if it had been possible, ye would have plucked out your own eyes, and have given them to me" (Gal. 4:15). I am sure that Paul had a serious visual problem.

When Paul wrote his Epistle to the Romans, he dictated it to a secretary. And at the conclusion of the letter, Paul said to the secretary, "Now if you want to put in your greetings, go ahead and do it." So in Romans 16:22 we have the secretary's salutation: "I Tertius, who wrote this epistle, salute you in the Lord."

However, when Paul wrote to the Galatians, he was angry. He had heard that they were mixing the gospel with law—and when that is done, the gospel of the grace of God is absolutely destroyed. He couldn't wait for a secretary to arrive—he just sat down and wrote to them himself. Because he didn't see clearly, he wrote with large letters.

I studied Shakespeare under a very skillful scholar who was partially blind. During class he would put the book right up to his nose and move it back and forth as he read. When he graded our papers, he would write his comments in large letters in the margin. His comments were brief because the words he wrote were so large. Apparently, Paul's writing was like that.

PAUL'S TESTIMONY

As many as desire to make a fair shew in the flesh, they constrain you to be circumcised; only lest they should suffer persecution for the cross of Christ [Gal. 6:12].

By exerting pressure and stressing circumcision among the Gentiles, the Judaizers hoped to escape the anger and wrath of Jews who were not believers. The Judaizers were the legalists of the day. Actually, you never get in trouble preaching legalism. It appeals to the natural man because law is given to curb him. A great many of us certainly feel that the old nature of the other man should be curbed.

I was talking to a man in a public place the other day when a boy drove about seventy-five miles an hour right through a dangerous intersection. This man wanted that boy arrested and put in jail. He wanted the boy to be forced to obey the law. This man rejects the grace of God—he is an unsaved man—but he certainly is for legalism. Every man wants the other man to obey the law.

Frankly, we also like a law we can obey. When I was a boy in school, I did some high jumping. In those days we started off with a three and one-half foot jump. When I jumped four feet, I had some difficulty. So when I practiced jumping, I always kept the bar at the four foot level. That is the way most people are about legalism. They want to be able to clear the hurdle, but they don't want it to be too high for them. Legalism is popular. The grace of God is unpopular. The human heart finds it repulsive. It is the offense of the Cross.

> **For neither they themselves who are circumcised keep the law; but desire to have you circumcised, that they may glory in your flesh [Gal. 6:13].**

By forcing the Gentiles to be circumcised the Judaizers would gain the credit for bringing them under the Law.

It is interesting that those who claim they live under the Law are not actually living by the Law. Many people who say that they live by the Sermon on the Mount are hypocrites. I know that to be true because of the experience I have had in the ministry.

Let me cite an experience I had many years ago at a luncheon at the Chamber of Commerce in Nashville, Tennessee. When I was a pastor in that city one of the elders in my church, who was a banker, was president of the Chamber of Commerce that year and invited me to speak to the group. I was a young pastor then—in fact, I was not yet married; it was my first pastorate. I arrived early and one of the officials was already at the speaker's table. He began talking with me, and I have never heard a man swear more than he did—and I've heard some who are experts at it. I didn't rebuke him, I just let him talk. Finally, in our conversation he asked me, "By the way, what's your racket?" I told him I was a preacher. He looked at me in amazement and asked, "Are you the speaker today?" When I said I was, he immediately began to tread water fast! He said, "Well, we're glad to have you, and I want you to know that I'm a Christian." That was certainly news, because I would never have suspected it by the way he was talking. Then he enlarged upon it. He told me he was an officer of a very fashionable church in Nashville. He told me about all the wonderful things that he did, then he concluded by saying, "The Sermon on the Mount is my religion." I said, "Fine. That's great!" I shook hands with him, then asked, "How are you coming with it?" He looked rather puzzled and asked, "What do you mean 'how am I coming with it?'" So I explained, "Well, you say the Sermon on the Mount is your religion, and I'd just like to know if you are living by it." He said he tried to. "But that is not what the Sermon on the Mount is all about. It puts down a pretty severe standard and it hasn't anything there about trying. You either do it or you don't do it. Now you say it's your religion so I assume you do it." He told me that he certainly tried. Then I began to push him a little. "Do you keep it?" He said, "I guess I do." "Well, let's see if you do. The Lord Jesus said that if you are angry with your brother you are guilty of murder. How do you make out on that one?" He hesitated, "Well, I might have a little trouble there, but I think I get by." "All right, let's try another commandment that the Lord Jesus lifted to the nth degree. He said if you so much as look upon a woman to lust after her, you're guilty of adultery. How about that one?" "Oh," he said, "that one would get me." I thought it would. I said, "Look, you're not keeping the Sermon on the Mount. If I were you I'd change my religion and get one I could keep." Do you see what he was? That man was a hypocrite. He went around telling others that he was living by the Sermon on the Mount and he was breaking it at every turn. He needed the grace of God. And there are multitudes of people just like him in many churches today. Paul mentions that with this tremendous statement:

But God forbid that I should glory, save in the cross of our Lord Jesus Christ, by whom the world is crucified unto me, and I unto the world [Gal. 6:14].

Between Paul and the world there was a cross. That should be the position of every believer today. That will have more to do with shaping your conduct than anything else. You will not boast about the fact that you are keeping the Sermon on the Mount, or that you belong to a certain church, or that you are a church officer, or a preacher, or a Sunday school teacher. You will not be able to *boast* of anything. You will just *glory* in the Cross and the One who died there.

For in Christ Jesus neither circumcision availeth any thing, nor uncircumcision, but a new creature [Gal. 6:15].

This brings us to the second kind of handwriting mentioned in these final verses.

Circumcision was the handwriting of religion and the Law. It was sort of a handwriting on the body. It served as a badge signifying that you belonged under the Abrahamic covenant. It never availed anything. Wearing a button or a pin, signifying that you belong to a lodge or a fraternity can become almost meaningless. "In Christ Jesus neither circumcision availeth any thing, nor uncircumcision"—uncircumcision is of no value either. These things carry no value whatsoever. There are folk today who like to boast of what great sinners they were before their conversion. Well, whether or not you have been circumcised—whatever was your state—is of no importance. The essential thing is: Has the Spirit of God come into your life and made you a new creature in Christ Jesus? This can come about *only* through faith in Christ.

You see, Paul would never have had any difficulty with the legalism of his day if he had presented the gospel as only a competitor in the field. Let me illustrate what I mean. We have an abundance of soaps on the market. Those who promote them tell us they will make you smell good or make you feel good or are kind to your skin. So let's you and me get out a new brand of soap, and we'll call it *Clean*, since getting you clean is the purpose of soap, and that seems to be the one thing the advertisers have forgotten. We'll start advertising it by claiming that it is the only soap that will make you clean. Our slogan will be "Buy Clean and get clean." Now that will get us in trouble immediately when we claim that it is the *only* soap that will get you clean. Manufacturers of other soaps will really begin to howl. But this is what Paul was claiming for the gospel. If he had said, "Juadism is good but Christianity is better," he wouldn't have been in trouble, because that's what advertisers say today—our product is better than other soaps on the market. That's competition. No one would dare say that their soap is the *only* soap that would do the job. Notice that Paul is not claiming that his soap is only a little better than the soap of Judaism; he is saying that Judaism is *nothing*, that circumcision is *nothing*, that whether you are circumcised or not circumcised is *nothing*. He is saying that only the writing of the Holy Spirit in your life, giving you a new nature, is essential. My friend, that is putting it on the line!

Now we come to the third and final handwriting presented to us in this section.

And as many as walk according to this rule, peace be on them, and mercy, and upon the Israel of God.

From henceforth let no man trouble me: for I bear in my body the marks of the Lord Jesus [Gal. 6:16–17].

Notice the word *marks*. Paul is saying, "I bear in my body the 'marks'"—the Greek word is *stigmata*—meaning 'scar marks.' If you want to see the handwriting of Jesus, look upon Paul's body. In 2 Corinthians 11:23–27 he tells us, "Are they ministers of Christ? (I speak as a fool) I am more; in labours more abundant, in stripes above measure, in prisons more frequent, in deaths oft. Of the Jews five times received I forty stripes save one. Thrice was I beaten with rods, once was I stoned, thrice I suffered shipwreck, a night and a day I have been in the deep; In journeyings often, in perils of waters, in perils of robbers, in perils by mine own countrymen, in perils by the heathen, in perils in the city, in perils in the wilderness, in perils in the sea, in perils among false brethren; In weariness and painfulness, in watchings often, in hunger and thirst, in fastings often, in cold and nakedness." The *stigmata* were the sufferings of Paul which he endured for the sake of the Lord Jesus.

In Paul's day *stigmata* was used in three ways. When a runaway slave was found and brought back to his master, he was branded on the forehead. Also soldiers who belonged to famous companies had the names of their commanders tattooed on their foreheads. Then, too, devotees of a pagan goddess (and there was much of this in Asia Minor and throughout the Roman Empire in Paul's day) had her name branded on their foreheads. Paul says, "I have on my body the *stigmata* of the Lord Jesus." He is saying this in effect, "I have written to you out of deep emotion and with great conviction. If you want to know if I truly believe what I have written and if these things are real in my own life, read my body—look at my scars."

I lived as a boy in west Texas before there were many fences, and we used to identify cattle by the brand of their owner. My friend, circumcision costs you nothing. It is only an outward sign. Paul says it is *nothing*, although he himself had been circumcised. But he bore the brand marks of the Lord Jesus upon his body and upon his life. I believe that in our day the Lord Jesus still stoops to write, not upon the shifting sands of the temple floor, but he writes upon the lives of those who are His own. His branding iron is on our hearts for eternity. Do we proudly wear His *stigmata*, willing to bear reproach for Jesus' sake?

Brethren, the grace of our Lord Jesus Christ be with your spirit. Amen [Gal. 6:18].

Paul concludes this marvelous epistle by commending the brethren to the grace of God.

BIBLIOGRAPHY
(Recommended for Further Study)

Cole, R. Alan. *The Epistle of Paul to the Galatians*. Grand Rapids, Michigan: Wm. B. Eerdmans Publishing Co., 1965.

DeHaan, M. R. *Galatians*. Grand Rapids, Michigan: Radio Bible Class, 1960.

Gromacki, Robert G. *Galatians: Stand Fast in Liberty*. Grand Rapids, Michigan: Baker Book House, 1979.

Hendriksen, William. *Exposition of Galatians*. Grand Rapids, Michigan: Baker Book House, 1968. (Comprehensive)

Hogg, C. F. and Vine, W. E. *The Epistle to the Galatians*. Grand Rapids, Michigan: Kregel Publications, 1922. (Excellent)

Ironside, H. A. *Expository Messages on the Epistle to the Galatians*. Neptune, New Jersey: Loizeaux Brothers, 1940. (All of his books are especially fine for young Christians)

Kelly, William. *Lectures on the Epistle to the Galatians*. Addison, Illinois: Bible Truth Publishers, n.d.

Kent, Homer A., Jr. *The Freedom of God's Sons: Studies in Galatians*. Grand Rapids, Michigan: Baker Book House, 1976. (Excellent for personal or group study)

Luther, Martin. *Commentary on Galatians*. 1525. Reprint. Grand Rapids, Michigan: Kregel Publications, n.d. (Abridged)

Ridderbos, Herman N. *The Epistle of Paul to the Galatians*. Grand Rapids, Michigan: Wm. B. Eerdmans Publishing Co., 1953.

Strauss, Lehman. *Devotional Studies in Galatians and Ephesians*. Neptune, New Jersey: Loizeaux Brothers, 1957.

Tenney, Merrill C. *Galatians: The Charter of Christian Liberty*. Grand

Rapids, Michigan: Wm. B. Eerdmans Publishing Co., 1954. (Excellent illustration of ten methods of Bible study)

Vaughan, Curtis. *Galatians: A Study Guide Commentary.* Grand Rapids, Michigan: Zondervan Publishing House, 1972.

Vos, Howard F. *Galatians—A Call to Christian Liberty.* Chicago, Illinois: Moody Press, 1971. (An excellent, inexpensive survey)

Wiersbe, Warren W. *Be Free (Galatians).* Wheaton, Illinois: Scripture Press (Victor Books), n.d.

Wuest, Kenneth S. *Galatians in the Greek New Testament for English Readers.* Grand Rapids, Michigan: Wm. B. Eerdmans Publishing Co., 1944.